Aesthetic Vedanta

the sacred path
of passionate love

Aesthetic Vedanta

the sacred path of passionate love

SWAMI B. V. TRIPURARI

MANDALA
publishing group

Mandala Publishing Group
103 Thomason Lane
Eugene, Oregon 97404
(541) 688–2258

Library of Congress Catalog Card Number: 97–66692
ISBN: 1–886069-14-X

Printed in the United States of America

To My Divine Guardians
A. C. Bhaktivedanta Swami Prabhupada
and Bhakti Raksaka Sridhara Maharaja

Contents

Foreword

The playful dance of beauteous love (*rāsa-līlā*) between divinity and humanity is one of the most sublime metaphors of India. It is the leitmotif of the devout followers of Lord Kṛṣṇa, whose dance with the enchanted gopīs (cowgirls) of Vṛndāvana is remembered in exquisite Sanskrit in the *Śrīmad-Bhāgavatam* (also called *Bhāgavata Purāṇa*). Here we can read of the heart-rending love spell he cast upon the villagers by his youthful beauty, unsurpassed charm, and extraordinary radiance, which irresistibly drew the gopīs closer and closer to him. Seeking to kindle their passionate longing for him still more, he played his magical flute whose unearthly sounds bewildered their minds, leaving in them only a single burning desire: to be absorbed in Śrī Kṛṣṇa, heedless of all else.

The divine Gopāla ("protector of the cows/earth"), who had incarnated to restore the moral order (*dharma*) and to light the flame of unconditional love in mature souls, embraced all equally. At the climax of Kṛṣṇa's love play, he, assuming the role of the lover perfectly, danced a dance of ecstatic abandon with all the gopīs simultaneously. And yet, each gopī was so flawlessly merged with him that they all were completely oblivious of each other, seeing only their beloved.

One gopī, the lovely Rādhā, has been singled out by the sages who recounted this great mythic dance because of her spiritual maturity. Her all-consuming, un-self-conscious love for the Lord has become the grand ideal guiding those who, knowing of the ultimate secret of the heart, seek the divine through the agency of feeling. The creative, erotic tension between Rādhā and Kṛṣṇa has served many generations of spiritual practitioners as a potent metaphor for their own inner struggle, yielding both the joy of union and the despair of apparent separation and leading to ever more profound love. The powerful myth of the *rāsa-līlā* is true for all times, because it captures the unique relationship that eternally exists between the divine and the human heart overflowing with transrational, rapturous love for the supreme person, the source of all beings and things.

As is the case with any true myth, the *rāsa-līlā* can be understood on many levels. The present book focuses on the aesthetic message: truth is beautiful and beauty is truthful. The West's encounter with India's spiritual heritage has largely occurred through the philosophical lens of Advaita Vedānta, notably the radical nondualist metaphysics of Śaṅkara (eighth century C.E.). While this lens offers many intriguing insights, it does not permit us to encounter the full range of Indic wisdom. In fact, it has considerably blinded us to the fact that living Vedānta has little to do with Śaṅkara's abstract system, which emphasizes discerning wisdom *(vijñāna)* but pays virtually no attention to the power of feeling, specifically love/devotion *(bhakti)*.

This book, like the other books authored by the erudite Swāmī Tripurāri, helps us catch up with historical reality. Focusing on the multivalent concept of *rasa,* he introduces the rich philosophy, theology, and spiritual practice of Acintya-Bhedābheda Vedānta, founded by the master of devotional ecstasy, Śrī Caitanya, who lived in the 16th century C.E. He shows that beauty has a place not only in the ordinary world of aesthetic experience but also and especially in the realm of spirituality.

Śrī Caitanya's school rejects the bland concept of a formless, unqualified Absolute (Brahman), as preached by Śaṅkara and others, replacing it with a teaching that does not deprive the divine of quality, form, and beauty. For Śrī Caitanya and his followers, *bhakti* is the ultimate aesthetic experience, or *rasa,* which is beauty and joy eclipsing all other emotions. This experience is quite different from conventional aesthetic experience, for it is not triggered by a material object (such as a painting or sculpture). Rather its source is the divine itself, and for this reason it also is truly truth-bearing and liberating. It alone has the power to lift the individual straight out of the self-imposed prison of egocentric thought and behavior.

Thus *bhakti-yoga,* the spiritual path of love/devotion, revolves around the cultivation of ecstatic self-surrender, yielding the graceful gift of *rasa*. The devotee reexperiences the divine *rāsa-līlā* in deep meditation, when the mind's walls have crumbled and the heart stands naked before the Beloved, whose sweetness (*mādhurya*) knows no end. Liberation in love is not mere isolation from the drama of ephemeral existence (*saṁsāra*) but freedom from the ego-personality and the empowerment to participate consciously and ecstatically in the eternal *līlā* (play) of the divine. The liberated devotee does not rest content with reaching the summit of spiritual practice but, seeing the divine in all beings and things, happily returns to the valley of life to bear witness to the supernal beauty in everything. In a way, he or she never leaves the valley but discovers the summit of spirituality amidst daily life: love melts down the distinction between sacred and profane, and in full bloom can be at least as potent a mind-harnessing tool as conventional yogic meditation. In love, all the energies of the soul are focused into a single laser beam that reaches across the gap between the artificial boundaries of the intellect, uniting the devotee's heart with the ever-pulsing heart of the Beloved.

We cannot fail to see the distinct flavor of Tantra in Gauḍīya Vedānta—not the flawed imitation Tantra of contemporary would-be seekers who confuse bliss with pleasure but the traditional Tantra that recognizes the transformative power of passion (*rāga*) directed toward the divine. Gauḍīya Vedānta is an integral part of the sweeping movement that significantly transformed the spiritual heritage of Hinduism, Buddhism, and Jainism. The Tantric adepts accomplished what the renowned historian of religion Mircea Eliade called a comprehensive "revalorization," leading to a whole new sensibility entailing a positive appraisal of the feminine element. This showed itself in many ways, and in Gauḍīya Vedānta found expression in a vigorous embrace of the dimension of feeling *(bhāva)*.

After a protracted period of intellectual aridity, epitomized by the religious abstraction of deism, we in the West are currently rediscovering the feminine principle on several levels. We are able to do so largely thanks to the epochal work of Carl Gustav Jung, who retrieved for our civilization the long-repressed notion of anima and with it the psychological energy it stands for. In this process of rediscovery, assimilation, and integration, the wisdom teachings of Gauḍīya Vedānta can serve us as a helpful mirror. Certainly anyone seriously concerned with realizing our species' full spiritual potential must consider the role and function of feeling. As the sages of India noted long ago, there are many ways to the One. But we must be careful to tread a genuine path lest we should end up in a desert of impotent concepts and heady experiences of no ultimate relevance. As wise pilgrims, we must make sure that our intellectual understanding is grounded in bodily reality and also that our mystical feelings are not mere self-indulgent emotions. Knowledge is valuable only to the degree that it reveals truth. Similarly, for love to truly be a life-transforming agency it must not be tainted by ignorance and selfishness.

Our contemporary struggle to discover a viable practical spirituality for ourselves, which not merely appeals to the mind but also satisfies the heart, can be greatly aided by Swāmī Tripurāri's lucid exposition of Gauḍīya Vedānta. Like his learned predecessors in the Gauḍīya tradition, he amply demonstrates through his fine discourse that love need not be irrational, merely pure.

GEORG FEUERSTEIN, PH. D.
Director of Yoga Research Center
Author of *Shambhala Encyclopedia of Yoga*
and numerous other books.

Preface

THE HIGHER ONE CLIMBS on the ladder of spiritual love, the more difficult it is to recognize that love, for love by its very nature hides itself. The *rāsa-līlā* is perhaps the best example of this. It is a very spiritually elevated account of the secret love affair of the Absolute. Yet outwardly it appears to be an description of humanity's lower nature.

The *rāsa-līlā* was originally revealed to a wide audience by Śukadeva Goswāmī, a sixteen-year-old adept who wandered the countryside naked, oblivious to the external world. He was the ideal person to speak about this confidential affair of the Absolute, for everyone knew that he had no interest in mundane life. Although the *rāsa-līlā* may appear to the uninformed to be an account of a material affair, Śukadeva's keen interest in it demonstrates its exalted spiritual nature.

Thousands of years later, Śrī Caitanya commissioned his principal disciples to broadcast the message of the *rāsa-līlā* to the entire world. While preoccupied with the love of Rādhā and Kṛṣṇa, he himself maintained the highest moral character. The character of his disciples was also beyond reproach. Śrī Caitanya maintained that the love of Rādhā and Kṛṣṇa is so pure that hearing about it can purify the hearts of even the vilest persons.

Śrī Caitanya is considered to be a combined incarnation of Rādhā and Kṛṣṇa, descending to the world to distribute the highest divine love. About him it is said:

"The brightest jewel
of sacred love in passion
is never given at any time.
Yet the most merciful
in this age of quarrel
gives it out to all.
May that golden-lion son of Śacī
manifest in your heart."[1]

This book was written in pursuit of the import of this verse. It seeks to inform the world, and especially the literate West, as to the significance of *rāsa-līlā* as seen through the eyes of Śrī Caitanya. In so doing, it appropriately brings attention to Śrī Caitanya, and thus the spiritual passageway to the mysterious land of love. It is there that the *rāsa-līlā* is perpetually performed.

The cover art for this book was done by the renowned Mahaveer Swami of Bikaner, Rajasthan. It depicts the gopīs singing in separation from Kṛṣṇa as found in the *Gopī-gītā*. Mahaveer's sensitive insights have contributed progressively to Indian miniature painting while retaining the tradition's essence. It was a pleasure to work with him and to see him embrace the ideals of the devotional path of Śrī Caitanya.

I am indebted in this effort first and foremost to my spiritual preceptor and other senior members of the Gauḍīya Vaiṣṇava *sampradāya* who have blessed me in my spiritual life as a *sādhaka*. Many persons have offered practical help and inspiration, and I am indebted to all of them as well. As for my personal friends and students who have been a part of this effort, I thank them not, for this would only distance us from one another.

Introduction

THERE IS A FINE LINE between myth and reality. The word myth can mean a story that expresses a certain truth allegorically or it can simply mean a falsehood. Since the time of Freud and Jung, it has become popular to search for significant psychological truths in myths. Yet even the most powerful myth is at best only an allegory; it is not itself truth in the sense of objective reality. It is never a true story.

For most of us, our reality is the world of our mind, informed by data gathered through our senses. This may be *our* reality, but how real is it? It certainly does not endure. Our instruments of perception, our senses, are imperfect to begin with, and thus the world of our mind informed by them may be more false than real. Hot, cold, happy, sad, good, and bad are mental notions relative to our sense perception. The same day is cold for one and hot for another, good for one, bad for another. We view the world through the glasses of our mental and sensual experience, yet ultimately these get in the way of truly experiencing.

According to Vedānta, that which we presently perceive to be reality is more akin to myth, a falsehood, while we ourselves, the experiencers, are units of reality—souls. The phenomenal world is no doubt real, but our perception of it is false, so false that it causes us to lose sight of our souls. The sense of the loss of soul that permeates our culture serves to underscore the mythical quality of our perception of reality. That which we perceive to be reality is rather an allegory for the true story: it is a reflection of the reality of the Absolute. Upon close examination, we will find that this reflection reveals much to us about ultimate reality.

What then is the true story? The true story is the so-called myth that leads us to our soul and thus to the real. Indeed, that myth may not be a myth at all, just as our mental and sensual perception of so-called reality may not be reality. The religious "myth" of the *rāsa-līlā* that this book is concerned with *is* the ultimate reality, and not merely a myth. It is an ultimate reality, however, that also confirms the value of humanity, especially its sensual and emotional aspects, for it informs us both that our sensuality has its origins in the Absolute and that the Absolute's expression of such is best facilitated within the human experience. In the *rāsa-līlā*, God enters humanity to celebrate his sensuality, thus confirming the feeling in all of us that our drive for the erotic is not something to be abolished. It is to be redirected away from the world and toward the Absolute appearing in its human-like expressions of Rādhā and Kṛṣṇa. In the *rāsa-līlā,* we discover divine humanism—where divinity validates the essence of humanity, and humanity speaks to us about that which divinity must embody in its fullest manifestation.

The *rāsa-līlā* is considered by many to be the greatest story ever told. It has been recorded in the sacred literature of India, retold by poets, depicted by artists, sung about and celebrated in music, philosophized about, and meditated upon for thousands of years. It is one of the cultural and spiritual gems of the civilized world. Had it not been for the *rāsa-līlā* of Rādhā and Kṛṣṇa, the rich religious tradition of Hinduism might have been effaced from the world during the Muslim domination of India. Although the Muslims cared little for Hinduism, they could not ignore the love story of Rādhā and Kṛṣṇa. The Moghuls in particular commissioned their artisans to depict it in art, and the Muslims were thus stopped short in their conquest by the force of divine beauty and love.[1] Enduring, charming, and profoundly mystical, the love story of Rādhā and Kṛṣṇa is capable of conquering kingdoms, even one as fortified as the mythical empire of our mind. This is so because it speaks deeply to the soul, yet in a language most suited to our sensual and mental preoccupations.

Although the love story of Rādhā and Kṛṣṇa has been analyzed on many levels—social, psychological, political, and so on—an effort is made herein to lay bare its most far-reaching implications: It is the truth that many have reasoned is synonymous with beauty, and it is the eternal drama in which the soul can realize its highest potential, living in love.

The title *Aesthetic Vedānta* is drawn from a phrase I coined in *Tattva-sandarbha: Sacred India's Philosophy of Ecstasy.* In the concluding remarks of that book, I referred to Jīva Goswāmī's philosophy as a "Vedānta of Aesthetics." Reflecting on this term later, I felt that although Śrī Jīva's philosophy is indeed such, a book with greater aesthetic content would be an appropriate sequel. Whereas *Tattva-sandarbha* reveals a meta–narrative giving rise to an ultimate reality of love and beauty, the present book describes that ultimate reality and the means to access it, and thus its aesthetic content is considerable. At the same time, I have demonstrated throughout that the aesthetic content centered on the love life of Rādhā and Kṛṣṇa is in essence what the Upaniṣads are pointing to—Vedānta. I have done this primarily through footnotes, wherein I have also highlighted prominent aesthetic features of the *rāsa-līlā* found in the original Sanskrit poetry.

Any attempt to establish a structured, logical exegesis of beauty is bound to meet with failure. An exegesis of ultimate spiritual beatitude is no exception. This is so because beauty and spiritual experience are nonrational and transrational respectively. This is not to say that spiritual beauty is unreasonable, but rather that it picks up where reason leaves off. Because in this world we speak the language of logic, we are restricted when we try to speak about spiritual experience. Should we enter the spiritual reality, however, the language of logic will be of little utility, for in the spiritual plane the language is love. Inasmuch as it points to the love and beauty that Rādhā and Kṛṣṇa personify, the logical exercise of Vedānta is in itself beneficial. Nevertheless, direct expressions of the experience of this love are often more compelling. As a result, even if logic falls short, as it inevitably must, the poetry of and about the experience of *rāsa-līlā* throughout this book will speak for itself. A single poem expressing spiritual experience can convey the essence of that experience more than volumes of tightly reasoned argumentation.

The middle chapter of this book consists of a rendering of the *rāsa-līlā*. The *rāsa-līlā* was originally narrated in the *Bhāgavata Purāṇa*, also known as the *Śrīmad-Bhāgavatam*, in five *adhyāyas* of the tenth canto. These five *adhyāyas* are considered to be the distilled essence of the Purāṇa. It would, however, be practically impossible to understand the significance of the *Bhāgavata Purāṇa* were one to turn immediately to these essential five chapters. As the *rāsa-līlā* within the Purāṇa is preceded by considerable philosophy, I have similarly set the stage for the narrative in this book with an introductory chapter entitled "Truth and Beauty." In this first chapter, the terms *Vedānta* and *aesthetics* are discussed in consideration of the popular notion that truth is beauty. In the course of the discussion, Jīva Goswāmī's spiritual preceptor, Śrī Rūpa Goswāmī, is introduced as a Vedāntist, aesthetician, and ultimate role model for the soul who desires to enter the eternal drama of Rādhā and Kṛṣṇa's love life.

In retelling the *rāsa-līlā,* I have in places made use of insights that are hidden in the Sanskrit text itself. These insights have been taken from the Sanskrit commentaries on the *rāsa-līlā* written by the followers of Śrī Caitanya. In addition to the insights these commentaries draw from the text, they also supply details from the *Viṣṇu* and *Harivaṁśa Purāṇas.* Moreover, the commentators offer a glimpse into the drama based on their own transcendental/emotional experiences derived from meditation on the text. Thus as presented in this rendering, the story line is interwoven with philosophy, a style used by my eternal preceptor, A. C. Bhaktivedānta Swāmī Prabhupāda in his famous "Kṛṣṇa books."[2]

The concluding chapter outlines the path of passionate love, from which the book's subtitle is derived. This chapter outlines the means to enter Rādhā and Kṛṣṇa's life of spiritual love. This overview is based on Rūpa Goswāmī's masterpiece, *Bhakti-rasāmṛta-sindhu*, and other important works of the followers of Śrī Caitanya. Its purpose is to show those attracted by the philosophical premise on which the story is based the practical steps one must take to leave one's mental myth behind and enter the reality of Rādhā and Kṛṣṇa.

In our times people look for a spiritual path that is pragmatic. How will it help me in my day-to-day life? How will it make the world a better place for me to live and raise my children? These are good questions. Indeed, the world is overburdened with strife, and our individual lives are affected by it either directly or indirectly, as no decent person can live peacefully knowing of the suffering of others. Famine, disease, political oppression, corporate exploitation, and environmental disaster are but a few of the symptoms indicating the diseased condition of the world. But what is the disease itself? It is selfish desire, the disease of the heart (*hṛd roga*). In the least, it is this disease that the *rāsa-līlā* seeks to address.

The *rāsa-līlā* is a tale of selflessness to the extreme hidden in an exterior of selfish love. That selfish love in which we are all involved and thus most eager to hear about is the context in which the ultimate in selflessness is couched. Such is the beauty and mystery of the *rāsa-līlā*. No story speaks more about that which we all need to hear to make the world a better place—selflessness properly centered on the perfect object of love.

CHAPTER ONE

Truth & Beauty

In a land of touchstone,
fully satisfied people crave one thing alone,
not fortune nor freedom, no care for fame,
but a taste for two syllables that make up his name.

Animate and inanimate all lost in his will,
what is it that enables them to move yet be still?
Love eternal, love divine, love of Kṛṣṇa so sublime,
the truth that is beauty in a realm beyond time.

Who knows that place at once knows all,
yet at the same time knows not at all,
for truth is beauty but beauty calls,
and calling, beauty bewilders us all.

IN HIS ACCEPTANCE ADDRESS for the Nobel prize in literature, Aleksandr Solzhenitsyn cited a Russian proverb: "One word of truth outweighs the whole world." He also quoted Dostoyevsky: "Beauty will save the world." If one word of truth outweighs the whole world, the world must be very false. But this truth is unpalatable, given the extent of beauty in this world. So much is this so that we cling to the beauty of the world, even when we are told the simple yet profound truth that it will not endure. How then will beauty save us, when attachment to it seems to be the cause of *saṁsāra*, suffering in rounds of repeated birth and death?

For Dostoyevsky, beauty will save us because its manifestation in art, literature, poetry, and the like is a semblance of the divine beauty that truth must ultimately personify. The aesthetic experiences of reading great literature, viewing a drama, and reciting poetry are experiences of the threshold of transcendence. Having tasted a drop of truth, we will be driven to drink deeply from its cup.

Yet is truth itself beautiful? The quest for the beauty of the world no doubt must be balanced with the harsh truth of its ephemeral nature. But there must be more to truth than this if it is to save us. The harsh truth of the ephemeral is its inability to deliver enduring beauty. This, however, is but "one word of truth." It no doubt outweighs the entire experience of the ephemeral world, but it is not the whole truth. And half truth, we are told, is worse than no truth at all. If we are to live in the light of truth, that truth must be *inherently beautiful*. It must possess the full face of beauty, which truth's mere triumph over falsity lacks. The beauty of the world is what makes life worth living, and this tells us that without beauty even truth is lifeless. If truth is merely the negation of the material world—*neti neti* cry the Upaniṣads[1]—can we live in the void that is thus created, forever silent and still? Realizing the emptiness in the world's apparent fullness is itself a profound fullness, but as the Buddha says, it is merely the fullness of emptiness. If we move from negative numbers to zero, then zero appears to have positive value. But are there positive numbers as well?

It is our quest for beauty—real, enduring beauty—that will save us from settling for only the few words of truth that render the world false. This quest will move us from zero to an infinity of positive values. It should drive us onward to the whole truth of infinite conscious beauty, about which one cannot say enough.[2] Śaṅkara's *advaita-vedānta* of "consciousness is truth, the world is false"[3] falls short. We must progress from this half-truth to the whole truth of the beauty of consciousness in its fullest expression, a beauty whose mere reflection is the charm of the world. It is this beauty, the reality behind the reflection, that India's sacred Upaniṣads and devotional Vedānta refer to when they speak of Kṛṣṇa. Śrī Kṛṣṇa is, in Hegel's terminology, "reality the beautiful"; in Upaniṣadic language, *raso vai saḥ*, "Kṛṣṇa is aesthetic experience— *rasa*."[4]

The Upaniṣads form the latter portion of the Vedas. The legendary Vyāsa's dissertation on the Upaniṣads is thus referred to as the *Vedānta-sūtra*, or concise words (*sūtra*) on the concluding portion (*anta*) of the Vedas. *Sūtra* also means thread, thus Vyāsa's *sūtras* are the threads that tie together the meaning of the Vedas. Over the centuries, commentators have explained the *sūtras* of Vedānta in different ways. Nonetheless, all of these commentators have agreed on a basic premise. This common ground constitutes a foundation for that which Aldous Huxley, following the lead of Leibnitz, called the "perennial philosophy."

As modern science reaches a general consensus amidst a variety of premises about the nature of reality, so too did the Vedāntists. Whether it be classical Newtonian physics or the shift to quantum mechanics, mainstream scientists continue to agree that matter is at the bottom of everything. Similarly, whether they follow Śaṅkara's *advaita-vedānta*, Rāmānuja's *viśiṣṭādvaita-vedānta*, Madhva's *dvaita*, or Śrī Caitanya's *acintya-bhedābheda*, all Vedāntists agree on one basic premise—that consciousness, not matter, is the ground of being. Still alive today, Vedānta philosophy has won the patronage of many of our world's greatest thinkers, decade after decade, century after century.[5]

While Vedānta refers to conclusive truth, aesthetics is the philosophy of beauty. In Western terminology, Vedānta is comparable to the Greek notion of noetics. In Western thought, noetics, derived from the Greek *noésis* (intelligence or thought), was for some time in opposition to aesthetics. The word *aesthetics* derives from the Greek *aisthésis*, or sensation. In ancient Greece, knowing was considered opposed to a life of sense indulgence. Vedānta appears to be in agreement with this proposal. A life of sense indulgence and material acquisition is not a life lived in pursuit of knowledge. Taking this line of reasoning perhaps too far, Aristotle and Plato did not have a very high opinion of beauty expressed in art and drama. By the middle of the 17th century, however, Western aesthetics had improved its lot, coming to be known as "the philosophy of beauty." By the 19th century, this became the standard definition of Western aesthetics, largely due to Hegel, who used it in his theory of art. In the twentieth century, the philosophy of beauty was pushed from behind the curtain into the limelight when Benedetto Croce, in his famous work *Estetica,* presented aesthetics as that branch of philosophy upon which all others are dependent. In the words of Will Durant, "Wisdom is a means; beauty of body and soul is an end."[6]

Indologists have used the term *aesthetics* to refer to India's dramatic theory and arts. This is not the same as Western aesthetics, which is a philosophical inquiry into the nature of beauty, a branch of epistemology that questions the objectivity and subjectivity of beauty. Indian aesthetics is, however, about beauty and its truth. Bharata Muni is the father of India's secular aesthetics. His *Bharata-nāṭya-śāstra* relates that at the beginning of the *tretā-yuga*, the second of the Hindus' four cosmic time cycles, humanity began to suffer from pride, and thus the joyful life became mixed with suffering. With a view to remedy this, the gods approached Brahmā, the creator. Brahmā then manifested drama, in which all of the arts are contained. Drama and its attendants, such as music, dance, and poetry, were thus intended to edify human society and uplift humanity morally and spiritually through aesthetic experience, which Bharata termed *rasa*.

The Sanskrit root meaning of *rasa* is taste or flavor, but when used in the context of dramatic theory it is usually rendered as aesthetic experience or aesthetic rapture. It is sometimes explained by Indian Sanskrit dramatic theorists as the feeling successfully conveyed from the heart of the poet through his mind and words to the *sa-hṛdaya,* or the reader with a sympathetic heart. It is the tangible yet elusive relishing of the arts, the experience of beauty.

When we view a dramatic performance or read poetry, we are one step removed from everyday life.

In the world of the arts, we relax and experience various emotions without the consequences that accompany them in the real world. Thus drama is a pleasurable experience, even when the play is a tragedy. Secular *rasa* is tasted as a peak emotional experience.[7] Peak emotional experiences within the dramatic world are not considered actual emotional life, but are a semblance of it. Yet from another perspective these peak experiences might also be considered a semblance of ultimate reality. One step removed from the world, these experiences have been compared to tasting the pure soul, flavored only by the latent impressions (*saṁskāras*) formed over previous lives.

Latent impressions form *vāsanā*, or desires, within our consciousness. These impressions are roughly analogous to the Western notion of instinct. When we view a dramatic performance, dominant emotions relative to our *saṁskāras* are portrayed through the characters and various props, as well as through the bodily expressions of the performers. Thus we experience a semblance of the dominant emotions of the characters. When the dominant emotions are further augmented by fleeting auxiliary emotions, the peak experience of *rasa* is produced within the viewer possessed of a sympathetic heart. Secular theorists conclude that one then experiences one's soul, a unit of pure consciousness free from worldly involvement, yet tainted still by the latent impressions within the soul. This is the experience of secular *rasa*, which is likened to the realization of ultimate reality by some, primarily *advaitins*.[8]

Bharata Muni called the dominant emotions *sthāyi-bhāvas*. He enumerated eight of them, which have the capacity to rule like kings over other fleeting emotions: love (*rati* or *śṛṅgāra*), laughter (*hāsya*), heroism (*vīra*), sorrow (*karuṇā*), astonishment (*adbhuta*), anger (*raudra*), aversion (*vibhatsa*), and fear (*bhaya*). Later thinkers such as Abhinavagupta added serenity (*śānta*), the emotionless emotion likened to Kant's "disinterested delight." One of these dominant emotions pervades any dramatic scene like the invisible scent of perfume.

The dominant emotion of a dramatic scene is portrayed through the characters and props, which have been labeled *vibhāvas*. The *vibhāvas* are thus determinants, or causal factors, in the production of *rasa*, as they reveal the dormant dominant emotion. In a dramatic scene, one of the characters, such as a male lover, would be the *viṣaya-ālambana-vibhāva*, or the object to which the dominant emotion (in this case *rati*, or love) is directed. His female beloved would then be the *āśraya-ālambana-vibhāva*, or the vessel of that love. Thus we have a subject/object relationship as a requirement for *rasa*. The props such as the moonlight, the scent of blossoming flowers, romantic music, and so on would be the *uddīpana-vibhāvas*, or excitants that stimulate the emotion of love. All of these *vibhāvas* serve to give expression to the dominant emotion. When the lover and beloved manifest bodily symptoms such as the exchange of loving glances and smiling, these outward symptoms of the dominant emotion are called *anubhāvas*; they serve to further express the dominant emotion. When, in addition to the above ingredients, fleeting auxiliary emotions, labeled *vyabhicāri-bhāvas* —shyness, jubilation, and pride—augment the dominant emotion, the secular *rasa* of *rati*, or love, is experienced by the appropriate audience. Bharata's other dominant emotions likewise produce their respective peak experiences, or *rasa*, in connection with the above ingredients.

When *advaitins* compare the experience of secular *rasa* to Brahman realization, the comparison falls short for a number of reasons. First of all, the secular experience of *rasa* lasts only as long as the dramatic scene, whereas realization of Brahman is eternal. From the perspective of monistic *advaita-vedānta*, Brahman is not an experience at all. Its realization is thought to dissolve the experience, the experienced, and the experiencer into one undifferentiated ultimate reality, devoid of sound, name, color, form, and so on. Thus for monists, ultimate reality is nothing like aesthetic *rasa*, for there is no scope in ultimate reality for the necessary ingredients of *rasa*. There is no subject/object relationship, nor any variegatedness. Yet because secular *rasa* is considered to move one temporarily away from one's material emotional makeup by allowing one to step back from it into the realm of the arts, it is thought to move one in the direction of the depersonalization that the monists' notion of Brahman realization requires.

No doubt ultimate reality requires that we efface our present egotistic identification with matter, which gives rise to our material personality and illusory individuality. Yet this is only half of the equation. If ultimate reality is beautiful, if it is *rasa* as the Upaniṣads declare, and if for us it is the experience of *rasa*, we must have a spiritual identity through which we can experience it.

Although the notion of *rasa* experienced in dramatic performance and poetry may uplift the soul by temporarily removing it from its everyday emotional life, it is not the *rasa* that is mentioned in the Upaniṣads. By experiencing this secular *rasa* of the arts, one's soul will not be fulfilled, for this secular *rasa* is not of the nature of Brahman.

Furthermore, if Brahman is *rasa*, and the experience of this *rasa* is our perfection, neither can *rasa* be the notion of ultimate reality posited by the *advaitins*. The *advaitins'* notion of ultimate beauty appears contentless, formless, colorless, nameless, and so on. The degree of beauty one can find in merely ending one's mental and sensual identity crisis is limited. Yet when this crisis ceases through the culture of self-realization, when we feel at one with all, in opposition to no one, real life begins. It is this real life in transcendence that we are concerned with, not merely ending *saṁsāra*. In this lies the potential for a truth that is inherently beautiful—the very world, person, and form of beauty.

At this point one must ask, can one relish beauty without form or image? Image and form are emblems of beauty. The canvas and the brush, the words and their order, make accessible the beauty of art and literature. Beauty itself is abstract, yet it requires form for its expression. If beauty is truth, it is as alive as truth is, and in order to express itself as it must, it requires form. From within the Hindu pantheon and beyond it, if we are to search within all cultures and their myths, it would be hard to find a better candidate for the form of ultimate beauty itself than Kṛṣṇa.

The idea of a transcendental form of the Absolute finds support in the Upaniṣads. *Vedānta-sūtra* states, "The Absolute [Brahman] does not have an ordinary form, for its form is itself. The conception of form with regard to the Absolute is not meaningless; rather, it is analogous to light [such as the sun] and its form. The *śruti* declares as well that the form of the Absolute is its very essence. Furthermore, the sacred literature demonstrates this, as does the tradition."[9] In these *sūtras*, the notion that the form of the Absolute is different from ultimate reality, and thus constituted of subtle matter, is refuted. The *sūtras* clearly state that the form of the Absolute is nondifferent from the Absolute, echoing the *śruti* in such statements as "Salutation to Kṛṣṇa, the destroyer of suffering, who is the form of eternity, knowledge and joy."[10]

When the *śrutis* state in other places that the Absolute has no form, they refer to the fact that its form is not material. This form is not different from itself, as our form is different from ourselves. Brahman's form is all-pervasive, all-knowing, within all, and so on. Thus although there is form to the Absolute, it is very different from our material form, which is limited in so many ways. Brahman's unlimited form is something we have no experience of, yet the Vedānta informs us how we might experience such a wonderful reality—the form of beauty, beauty personified. In *Gopāla-tāpanīya Upaniṣad*, we find a description of this form as the object of meditation. "Meditate upon the Absolute as having eyes like the fully blossomed white lotus, with a body colored like rain clouds, wrapped in garments resembling lightning, with two hands bestowing ultimate knowledge [devotion]. Around his neck is a garland of forest flowers."[11] This is not a mentally conceived form for the convenience of meditation on a formless Absolute, but rather Brahman itself. Only meditation upon Brahman can bring realization of Brahman.

The Upaniṣads so declare the form of the Absolute to be the Absolute itself, and the sacred literature, as well as the tradition, demonstrates the same. In the *Śrīmad-Bhāgavatam,* the *śruti's* statements about the form of the Absolute are made concrete in the person of Kṛṣṇa. In the tenth canto of the *Śrīmad-Bhāgavatam*, in which the *līlās* of Kṛṣṇa are portrayed, the all-pervading nature of Kṛṣṇa's form is demonstrated repeatedly.[12]

Setting sacred literature and the logic for adhering to its conclusions aside, is there any other logic that supports the notion of a concrete Absolute of unlimited form? While the highest form of divine revelation must be free from sectarianism and thus represent the greatest generality, it must also possess the greatest wealth of positive content.

The Russian mystic and philosopher Vladimir Solovyov has coined the phrase "positive universality" in his attempt to describe the Absolute. He conceives of positive universality in contradistinction to the absence of all determinate properties and distinctive features. He opines in concert with the Upaniṣads that in seeking a universal religion and ultimate spiritual reality, it is insufficient to merely do away with all distinctive features of the Absolute. This is so because in doing so we reach at best only the lowest common denominator of religion. We arrive at the minimum of religious content. Such an abstract form of religion under any name, he reasons, leads ultimately to nihilism and atheism. Are we not threatened today with such in the guise of postmodern relativism and pluralism?

Solovyov would have us take a step forward. Acknowledging the general religious principle that constitutes our common religious ground, he asked his audience to go higher. "The richer, the more alive and concrete a religious form is, the higher it is. The perfect religion is not the one that is equally contained in all religions [the indifferent foundation of religion]; the perfect religion is one that possesses and contains within itself all religions [the complete religious synthesis]."[13] As we shall see, this is the meaning of "Kṛṣṇa," in which all forms of love find transcendental expression.

In devotion to Kṛṣṇa, we do not encounter the fanaticism that insists on only one spiritual revelation, for Kṛṣṇa includes all forms of the Godhead and thus all varieties of love of God.[14] Nor do we encounter the abstract rationalism that evaporates the essence of religion into a fog of indeterminate concepts, fusing all religious forms into a formless, colorless, impotent generality or void.

The Sanskrit syllable *kṛṣ*, from which the name Kṛṣṇa is derived, denotes existence. The suffix *na* suggests happiness. Thus "Kṛṣṇa" indicates the most blissful existence. *Kṛṣ* also grammatically denotes "to draw near," and *na* to renounce. Kṛṣṇa is that ultimate happiness, the beauty that draws all near to himself, causing us to leave the unhappiness of material attachment behind. Charming Kṛṣṇa of sweet form, sweet flute, sweet play, and sweet love is the concrete form of beauty of which the abstract language of the Upaniṣads speak. He is the form of beauty, without which the experience of beauty in transcendence is but half the truth. With the concept of Kṛṣṇa in mind, we mine a particularly rich vein of Vedānta philosophy, that of Gauḍīya Vedānta. *Gauḍīya* refers to Śrī Caitanya, who appeared in Gauḍadeśa, West Bengal. His extraordinary ecstasy and divine love have been explained in terms of Vedānta by Śrī Jīva Goswāmī. Śrī Jīva's guru, Rūpa Goswāmī, explained the same in terms of aesthetics. Thus Gauḍīya Vedānta may as well be termed aesthetic Vedānta.

Aesthetic Vedānta posits an inconceivable subject/object relationship, a relationship between God and soul that does not compromise the nondual nature of the Absolute. God is one. He is joy.[15] Yet for the sake of functioning, and thus tasting his own nature, he is two. This dyad is really a unity, a dynamic unity that is both the potent source and potency, energetic source and energy, *śaktimān* and *śakti*. There is no meaning to an energetic source that has no energy. Nor is it meaningful to speak of energy that is not generated from, and inherent within, an energetic source. Kṛṣṇa is thus energetic source and energy, Kṛṣṇa and Rādhā, respectively.

> *The water increases the beauty of the lotus,*
> *and the lotus increases the beauty of the water;*
> *both the water and the lotus enhance the charm of the lake.*

The bracelet is beautified by the jewel
and the jewel by the bracelet,
and both combine to increase the beauty of the hand.
So it is with Rādhā and Kṛṣṇa;
each of them increases each other's beauty
and together they augment the glories of Vraja.[16]

Kṛṣṇa is *rasa,* aesthetic experience, and he is *rasika,* the greatest connoisseur of aesthetic experience. Rādhā is the outpouring of this internal unity of *rasa* and *rasika.* The union of Rādhā and Kṛṣṇa has been compared to the union of an iron rod and fire. In such a union, the iron remains iron and the fire remains fire, yet the two become one. In the eternal function of *līlā,* or divine play, Kṛṣṇa fully tastes himself through his primal energy, Rādhā. Rādhā gives life to Kṛṣṇa as energy brings the energetic source to life. As sugarcane cannot taste itself, similarly the tasting of the Absolute *(rasa)* necessitates such a dynamic, nondual Absolute. The effect of the Absolute tasting itself through its essential *śaktis*[17] is the creation of the phenomenal world and all souls' apparent relationship with it.[18] When the Absolute (Kṛṣṇa) relates with the phenomenal world, this act of grace attracts all souls to unite with him, enter his divine play, and experience *rasa* beyond the confines of the phenomenal world.[19]

Whereas Śaṅkara's Brahman is still and quiet, the Brahman of Gauḍīya Vedānta theology is full of sound and movement that constitutes the celebration of its fullness. Such an understanding is impossible in Śaṅkara's *advaita-vedānta*, in which the individual soul is considered nondifferent in every respect from the Absolute, the phenomenal world does not ultimately exist, and the Absolute is devoid of potency. For aestheticians who align themselves with Śaṅkara's *advaita-vedānta*, aesthetics applies only to a world that is surrealistic, and not to reality, either relative or absolute. For the Gauḍīyas, however, beauty and truth are truly synonymous. In this school, where Vedānta reaches the mountain peak of truth, aesthetics dance us down the other side into the valley of ultimate beauty.

Rūpa Goswāmī, whose very name (*rūpa*) means both beauty and form, was the foremost spokesperson for the Gauḍīyas' aesthetic theory of transcendental *rasa*. His disciple, Śrī Jīva Goswāmī, was this school's foremost Vedāntin. Śrī Rūpa begins his magnum opus, *Bhakti-rasāmṛta-sindhu*, by offering respect to Kṛṣṇa, describing him as the emporium of *rasa*.[20] Of the many who have insisted that truth is beauty, from Hegel, Croce, Keats, and other aesthetic philosophers in the West to Abhinavagupta, Bhoja, Viśvanātha Kavirāja, and the like in the East, only Rūpa Goswāmī has explained in detail what that absolute beauty is like. Rūpa Goswāmī and his subsequent followers have blessed human society with the most concrete and extraordinarily detailed explanation of the beauty of divinity, such that all other descriptions are vague in comparison. Their mystic descriptions are so detailed as to the nature of an ultimate experience of love and beauty that one is compelled to believe them merely on account of the sheer magnitude of the information they provide. That their descriptions of ultimate beauty are at the same time so grounded in philosophy, so well-reasoned, and that the Goswāmīs' lives are examples of extraordinary states of ecstasy adds to their credibility.

In providing information about the truth that is beauty (*rasa*), Rūpa Goswāmī differs considerably from secular *rasa* theorists. While in secular aesthetics, devotion to God portrayed in drama is not considered to have the potential to produce *rasa*, Rūpa Goswāmī claimed that *bhakti*, devotion to Kṛṣṇa, is the only true and enduring aesthetic experience—*bhakti-rasa*. For Śrī Rūpa it involved not merely dismantling the material ego as secular aesthetics is considered helpful in doing, but promoting one's spiritual individuality, affording entrance into the eternal drama of the Absolute—Kṛṣṇa *līlā*.

The *līlā*, or divine play of God, is not easy to comprehend, and the *līlā* of Kṛṣṇa is all the more difficult. Being play, it is beyond comprehension, rhyme beyond reason. Yet it is not unreasonable. That God "plays" is not a notion outside Western thought. Plato indicated it indirectly when he described human beings as God's "toys"—"and with regard to the best in us, that is what we really are."[21] We are thought by Plato to have been the verse of God's poetry, although responsible for what we are at present. This implies both action under the law of karma as well as God's life beyond the karmic realm of cause and effect. The phenomenal world is the play of God, and at the same time he has his own life transcendent to the phenomenal world. As Meister Eckhart says, "This play was played eternally before all creatures." Vedānta tells us that the phenomenal world is caused by nothing more than this play of God.[22] Thus the Absolute moves out of joy in aesthetic rapture.

If we do play, such play arises out of accumulated power, either the power of others or that of our own. As children, our play arises out of the power base of our elders. In adult life, we play as much as we can afford to. If we play without concern for accumulating a power base, we suffer in the long run. If children forgo education, from which one acquires the power of knowledge, their potential for future play is damaged. Thus play requires power, and that expression of the Absolute in which play alone is depicted is also the most powerful.

We are obliged to work as a result of the need born of forgetfulness of our own nature, a need arising out of material identification. This is the karmic struggle. The Absolute, on the other hand, along with those who forget him not, play rather than work. Illusioned souls, ignorant of their potential for relationship with the Absolute, work out of a perceived necessity, while the liberated play not because of what they need, but because of what they are.

In Sanskrit, gods are called *devas.* The Sanskrit root for the word *deva* is *div*, which means "to play." Gods play, and the most powerful God does nothing else. Kṛṣṇa has described himself thus in the *Bhagavad-gīta*:

> *O son of Pṛthā,*
> *there's nothing in all the three worlds that I must do,*
> *nothing I need to attain,*
> *yet still I act.*[23]

Of all the Gods, no one plays more than Kṛṣṇa. Kṛṣṇa lives forever in the magical land of his own fantasy. He does whatever he wants, whenever he wants, and yet in so acting he is loved by all, for he is never proud or vindictive. He lives not in a palace seated on a throne, but in a common rural setting, accessible to all. Only when the occasional demon enters his play are we reminded of his Godhood. Although he descends to earth to destroy the miscreants, his Vraja *līlā* has no purpose, relatively no connection with this aspect of his mission. Thus Vraja Kṛṣṇa is not an *avatāra*, descending with a mission, but the *avatārī*, the source of all *avatāras,* who has no mission to fulfill. Carefree, beautiful, inviting, he embodies all that is unnecessary in life, its luxuries and leisure, without which life would not be worth living. In all of Kṛṣṇa's play, he stands on equal footing with his cowherd friends and lovers, and thus he invites all souls to play with him as well. If we enter his life, we too will play in aesthetic rapture.

Kṛṣṇa is joy and we are joyful when we have a relationship with him. This relationship is *rasa*. *Rasa* expresses itself in the context of *līlā*. Kṛṣṇa *līlā* is then the ultimate drama, and it is in this drama that we can understand the *rasa* of the Upaniṣads. Rūpa Goswāmī's position on this is so firm that, representing him a century later, Viśvanātha Cakravartī Ṭhākura insisted that *rasa* does not appear at all in worldly drama.[24] Rūpa Goswāmī himself has said, "All other emotions (other than *kṛṣṇa-rati*) are meaningless."[25] For Śrī Rūpa, secular aesthetics has no soul, and *bhakti-rasa* alone is true beauty. *Rasa* is Kṛṣṇa, and *rasa* is the true experience of Kṛṣṇa.

Rūpa Goswāmī adjusted aesthetic theory further in terms of his emphasis on the dominant emotion. For Śrī Rūpa, the dominant emotion is not a product of the material experience. Rūpa Goswāmī's dominant emotion descends through grace into the heart of a devotee of Kṛṣṇa. It is the *premāṅkura,* or the sprout of love of Kṛṣṇa. It is one ray of the sun of love of Kṛṣṇa, *prema-sūryāṁśu,* and is constituted of Kṛṣṇa's internal spiritual energy. Thus for Śrī Rūpa, the intensification of the dominant emotion is *rasa.* Just as the ocean sends forth clouds, which in turn pour water back into the ocean, causing it to swell, the transcendental dominant emotion produces the rain clouds of the ingredients of *rasa*, which in turn nourish the dominant emotion, causing it to ascend to the peak experience of *rasa.*

In Rūpa Goswāmī's *bhakti-rasa*, Kṛṣṇa is the *viṣaya*, the perfect object of love. His devotee is the *āśraya,* or vessel of that love. *Kṛṣṇa-rati,* or Kṛṣṇa-directed love, is the dominant emotion. The *vibhāvas, anubhāvas,* and *vyabhicāri-bhāvas* bring the dominant emotion of *kṛṣṇa-rati* to the state of *rasa* in the hearts of Kṛṣṇa's devotees through the culture of devotion to him. *Kṛṣṇa-rati* causes the soul to view Kṛṣṇa with eyes of love, and thus in effect transform him, and all that is associated with him, into excitants that intensify *kṛṣṇa-rati.* Subsequently, *kṛṣṇa-rati* manifests in outward expression in the devotee as well as auxiliary emotions and involuntary movements known as *sāttvika-bhāvas*,[26] thus intensifying the dominant emotion into *rasa*.

In Śrī Rūpa's doctrine, the viewer of the ultimate drama of Kṛṣṇa *līlā* actually enters into that drama in meditation, living and loving in eternity. Indeed, properly understood, participation in the *līlā* of Kṛṣṇa is the ultimate manifestation of ecstatic love. *Bhakti-rasa* is the dynamic union of soul and God in love.

Kṛṣṇa is that notion of God in which the greatest potential for transcendental love can be realized. Kṛṣṇa and his associates, and especially the gopīs, his cowherd girlfriends, cherish the most intimate aesthetic rapture. Kṛṣṇa is beauty, and all things—even that which is immoral from a worldly point of view—become beautiful in relation to him. This is so, Śrī Rūpa posits, because love directed to Kṛṣṇa is love properly centered, while worldly love is no more than the demands of the material senses and mind driving the eternal soul to relate with another's outward appearance. In worldly love, the inherent drive or potential for love within the soul and the object of love are categorically different.

The mind is attracted to "another" with whom we identify. This self-identification is fundamental to the relationship of love. When we think of another as ours, whether it be a person or an object, the mental identification expressed as "mine" serves to illustrate that love is based in the self, the soul.[27] We units of individual consciousness are rooted in the ground of being, Brahman, who in its ultimate expression of joy is Kṛṣṇa. While reality is Kṛṣṇa-centered love, the illusory life in the material world is love in the shadow, illicit by way of its being off-center. Although love in reality is centered in consciousness, we do not understand this fact, nor the fact that the self is derived from Kṛṣṇa. As such, the love of and within the phenomenal world is off-center. Vedānta, then, affords us a proper conceptual orientation so that true love and beauty can be realized.

While Kṛṣṇa, or God, in any of his incarnations is the perfect object of love from the viewpoint of Vedānta (truth), Kṛṣṇa alone is the perfect object of love when we gaze through the eyeglass of aesthetics (beauty). A sampling of aesthetic analysis with regard to the ideal lover will help to illustrate this point. In

Indian aesthetics, there are 4 ideal male personality types, or heroes (*nāyakas*). According to Rūpa Goswāmī, these 4 are further considered in terms of their being perfect (*pūrṇa*), more perfect (*pūrṇatara*), and most perfect (*pūrṇatama*). Thus the 4 types become 12. These 12 are further categorized in terms of married heroes (*pati*) and paramour lovers (*upapati*), thus making 24 varieties of heroes. These 24 are further considered with regard to four dispositions: impartial, faithful, bold, and cunning. When we speak of Kṛṣṇa, we are speaking about the ultimate lover, God, who embodies all 96 of these heroes. This is demonstrated in the writing of Śrī Rūpa Goswāmī with reference to sacred literature, replete with examples from the recorded history of Śrī Kṛṣṇa's earthly appearance.

Śrī Rūpa mentions 64 principal qualities of Kṛṣṇa. He explains that people in general can possess up to 50 of these qualities in minute quantities, while gods like Brahmā and Śiva possess up to 55 of them. Viṣṇu possesses 60 of these principal qualities, and the 4 remaining qualities are unique to Kṛṣṇa. These final 4 qualities have a particular relationship with charm and sweetness (*mādhurya*). Kṛṣṇa has the form of sweetness (*rūpa-mādhurya*), he plays the sweet flute (*veṇu-mādhurya*), his pastimes are full of sweetness (*līlā-mādhurya*), and his love of the gopīs is of unrivaled sweetness (*prema-mādhurya*). No other expression of God embodies such charm. Rūpa Goswāmī has demonstrated that, objectively speaking, Kṛṣṇa's form, flute playing, pastimes, and love in particular have no comparison in the material universe and beyond. Thus Kṛṣṇa of dark complexion (*śyāma*), the color that according to aesthetics corresponds with the inner emotion of conjugal love, is not a sectarian God. He is objectively the embodiment of all potential for love. If one were to combine all that would be necessary from aesthetic analysis to make the perfect lover, that person would be Kṛṣṇa, the all-attractive, and in the language of Śrī Jīva Goswāmī, the irresistible. In his *Ujjvala-nīlamaṇi*, Śrī Rūpa has demonstrated as well that Śrī Rādhā is the perfect heroine, embodying the essence of aesthetic science's 360 types of heroines.

Rūpa Goswāmī chose to delineate his theory of aesthetic Vedānta through the medium of the *Bhāgavata Purāṇa*, which is by far the most popular of all the Purāṇas. It enjoys this status both within India and abroad. It was the first Purāṇa ever to be translated into English. Bengal alone has more than 40 translations of the text. It has been translated into thousands of Indian dialects, including aboriginal languages. Even the great Moghul emperor Akbar humbled himself before the *Bhāgavata Purāṇa* as represented by the Vṛṇdāvana Goswāmīs. The *Bhāgavata Purāṇa* is itself a Vedānta of aesthetics. It is considered a commentary on the *Vedānta-sūtra* by the *sūtra*'s compiler.[28] The *Padma Purāṇa* states that when the *Bhāgavatam* is recited, the Vedas, Purāṇas, and *Vedānta-sūtra* assemble to hear it.[29] The text describes itself as the essence of the *śruti*, the Upaniṣads.[30] Because of its Vedāntic nature, its aesthetic content is an advocacy of an ultimate reality that is the form of beauty, the ultimate form of aesthetic experience. It is the ripened fruit of the wish-fulfilling tree of Vedic knowledge, and thus a book of philosophy.

At the same time, *Śrīmad-Bhāgavatam* is a literary masterpiece of Sanskrit poetics. With respect to relish, suggestive poetry, embellishments, lyric poetry, and metre, its position is unique within the Purāṇic literature of India. It is a book of aesthetic experience that the reader is to drink from until he is rendered unconscious, only to rise and drink again its intoxicating elixir of *rasa*.[31]

Rūpa Goswāmī is considered the tradition's expert on aesthetic rapture. His seminal *Bhakti-rasāmṛta-sindhu*, "The Nectar Ocean of *Bhakti-Rasa*," as well as its sequel, *Ujjvala-nīlamaṇi*, are both based squarely on *Śrīmad-Bhāgavatam*, as are the works of Śrī Rūpa's elder brother Sanātana Goswāmī. Śrī Sanātana wrote a commentary on the tenth canto of *Śrīmad-Bhāgavatam*, entitled *Vaiṣṇava-toṣaṇī*. He also wrote *Bṛhad-Bhāgavatāmṛta*, in which he explains the significance of *Śrīmad-Bhāgavatam*. Śrī Rūpa's disciple, Jīva Goswāmī, wrote a full commentary on the *Bhāgavatam* entitled *Krama-sandarbha*, a gloss on Sanātana Goswāmī's commentary entitled *Laghu-toṣaṇī*, as well as a six-part treatise on the *Bhāgavatam* itself, entitled *Ṣaṭ-sandarbha*. Jīva Goswāmī also wrote a poetic rendering of the *Bhāgavatam*'s tenth canto entitled *Gopāla Campū*. Later, in the same tradition, Viśvanātha Cakravartī wrote a commentary on the *Bhāgavatam*. These scholars and devotees of the *Bhāgavatam* were also players in the text itself. If Vyāsa wrote the *Bhāgavata*, as the tradition claims, Śrī Rūpa, Sanātana, Śrī Jīva, and Viśvanātha were actors in the script of Kṛṣṇa's divine *līlā* that forms the essence of the text.

Appearing as mendicant philosophers in this world, these Goswāmīs[32] are eternal members of Kṛṣṇa's *rāsa* dance of love. Real players in the eternal drama, they appeared here as followers of Śrī Caitanya, whom they recognized as Kṛṣṇa, disguised by the emotions *(bhāva)* of his own devotee—the best devotee, Śrī Rādhā. Śrī Caitanya came both to teach devotion to Kṛṣṇa, *bhakti-rasa*, and to experience its essence himself.

According to the Goswāmīs, when the ultimate entity searches out his own beauty, he adopts the emotions of the one most devoted to him, who knows his beauty better than any other. Rādhā is Kṛṣṇa's eternal consort, the feminine counterwhole of the ultimate entity—Śrī Kṛṣṇa. In Śrī Rādhā, both deity and perfection of devotion reside. When Kṛṣṇa appears as Śrī Caitanya, it is the Rādhā in this appearance of Kṛṣṇa that the Goswāmīs are most concerned with. They themselves are her maidservants in transcendence *(mañjarī-gopīs)*, and thus their explanation of *Śrīmad-Bhāgavatam* is necessarily insightful and esoteric.

The *Bhāgavata Purāṇa* consists of 12 cantos and deals with ten subjects, termed *tattvas*, or ontological realities. The tenth *tattva* is the shelter of the other nine. The nine sheltered *tattvas* derive their value from the tenth. The shelter-giving *tattva* is dealt with throughout the Purāṇa, yet is most extensively discussed in the tenth canto. This ultimate *tattva* is Śrī Kṛṣṇa, upon whom the other *tattvas* depend.

From the Vedāntic point of view, Kṛṣṇa is the shelter of all, including Śrī Rādhā. From the aesthetic angle, however, Kṛṣṇa is the object of love (*viṣaya*) and Rādhā is the vessel (*āśraya*) of perfect love. Thus from aesthetic analysis, Rādhā is love's embodiment, whom we are to follow if we are to love Kṛṣṇa in the most comprehensive manner. Yet because she is so, the Goswāmīs have found reason to make her, along with Kṛṣṇa, the very object of their love[33] and thus for those who choose to follow in their footsteps, the Goswāmīs themselves are the receptacles of the highest love. They are the example of love that we are to follow, should we be interested in experiencing the deepest love, the sweetest aesthetic rapture in the land of beauty. As we shall see in the final chapter of this book, the Goswāmīs are role models for the spiritual aspirant, outwardly in terms of their example as renunciate-devotees, as well as internally in terms of their gopī roles in the inner world of Kṛṣṇa *līlā*.

The *Śrīmad-Bhāgavatam*'s tenth canto gives us a glimpse into the eternal world of Rādhā-Kṛṣṇa and their associates. In chapters 29 through 33, the *rāsa-līlā* of Rādhā-Kṛṣṇa and the gopīs is described. It is advised by the Goswāmīs that in order to appreciate the transcendental significance of this esoteric section of the text, one should accept the guidance of a preceptor and under his or her direction study the *Bhāgavatam* in its entirety. One must become a Vedāntist to appreciate the aesthetic reality described in these chapters. Without doing so, one runs the risk of misinterpreting the divine *līlā* of Rādhā-Kṛṣṇa, equating it with the mundane experience of amorous love.

At a glance, Rādhā-Kṛṣṇa's *rāsa-līlā* appears to be no more than a beautiful, poetic love story. At closer examination, it appears to be a metaphor for both a means (*sādhana*) and end (*sādhya*) of transcendental culture, culminating in liberation from *saṁsāra*. Looking at Rādhā-Kṛṣṇa's *rāsa-līlā* through the eyes of the

Goswāmīs, however, takes us a giant step further, from the door of transcendence into the house of *bhakti*. While material love is sensuality centered upon falsehood, the half-truth of liberation from *saṁsāra* is devoid of sensuality. What the Goswāmīs have revealed is the best of both. Theirs is a suprasensual experience, devoid of material inebrieties, centered upon the perfect object of love—ultimate truth and beauty personified.

For the Goswāmīs, *bhakti-rasa* has five direct expressions in relation to Kṛṣṇa and seven indirect expressions. The five direct varieties of *bhakti-rasa* parallel the five primary types of loving exchanges we know of from our material experience. Thus the dominant emotion of Kṛṣṇa-directed love culminating in *bhakti-rasa* manifests either as passive love (*śānta*), servitorship (*dāsya*), fraternity (*sakhya*), parental love (*vātsalya*), or in the optimum, as in the case of the gopīs, conjugal love (*mādhurya*).

Passive love is the ground floor of Rūpa Goswāmī's house of transcendent *bhakti-rasa*, conjugal love the penthouse suite. In between these two stories of aesthetic rapture are the other dominant emotions of servitude, fraternity, and parenthood. The lobby is freedom from material desire. Although liberation is a requirement for entering the house of *bhakti*,[34] it is so only in the sense that it is a step all must tread in order to enter *bhakti-rasa*. *Bhakti-rasa* takes place in a post-liberated ultimate reality. Upon realizing oneself in terms of identification with Brahman through the culture of one of these Kṛṣṇa-directed emotions, one proceeds to experience the fullness of the particular variety of *bhakti-rasa* that one has cultivated from the start.

From passive love to servitude, the soul's love for Kṛṣṇa intensifies from neutral love to relational love. Servitude includes the basic elements of passive love, with the addition of personal service to Kṛṣṇa. Fraternity intensifies further, such that while all of the essential elements of servitude and passive love are present, intimacy develops. In this aesthetic experience, the soul shares equal footing with Kṛṣṇa within the drama of his eternal *līlā*. The friends of Kṛṣṇa love him so intensely that their love overrides any sense of his superiority. Parental love is still more intense. Embracing all that is essential in the other dominant emotions, parental love further includes a sense of protectiveness for Kṛṣṇa. In this variety of *bhakti-rasa*, Kṛṣṇa becomes the dependent of his devotees, and thus in aesthetic Vedānta, God, the unborn parent of all, has parents of his own. Here the Christian concept of God as father is reversed as Kṛṣṇa becomes the son of his devotee! No doubt the love of the parent for the child is more intense and involves greater sacrifice and love than that of child for parent. Beyond parental love for Kṛṣṇa, love takes one more step in which the soul embraces the Absolute as only a lover can.

Passive love, servitude, fraternity, parental love, and conjugal love thus form the direct modes of loving Kṛṣṇa within *bhakti-rasa*. Rūpa Goswāmī's seven indirect modes of *bhakti-rasa* are humor, disgust, fear, heroism, compassion, wonder, and anger, which correspond to the secular aestheticians' seven *rasas* other than *rati* (conjugal love). For Śrī Rūpa, these seven, when nourished by one of the direct forms of *kṛṣṇa-rati*, attain the status of *rasa* themselves.

One can easily understand how our material lives in search of love are a reflection of Rūpa Goswāmī's ultimate reality, in which the structure of love remains in place, while the foundation alone is changed. The foundation of transcendental love is selflessness; the foundation of mundane love is selfishness. The latter is an ugly, flickering product of the mind; the former the beautiful, eternal life of the soul.

It may be somewhat bewildering how Kṛṣṇa can be the all-pervasive reality and yet partake in pastimes that involve somehow moving about beyond the confines of time and space. Moreover, his liberated devotees, who appear as his admirers, servitors, friends, parents, and lovers, are not even aware that he is the ultimate truth. Should such an awareness cross their minds, though it may be true, it would be an impediment to their intimacy with him. And so it is for Kṛṣṇa as well. Lost in a world of transcendental aesthetics, even Kṛṣṇa, under the influence of his own potency, does not know he is the truth. For, to the extent that Kṛṣṇa is aware that he is the truth, that truth loses its beauty and charm. If this is the case, how then can *we* "know" this truth? Such is Gauḍīya Vedānta, through which we too can one day leave the world of knowing behind and enter the truth that is beauty.

The beauty of Kṛṣṇa is in the suppression of his grandeur as God. This is also his claim to ultimacy, not only over all souls, but over all of his *avatāras*, or incarnations, as well. Although Kṛṣṇa's humanness has brought his ultimacy into question, such objections are not well thought out. Because the Absolute's ultimate objective is play for its own sake, simplicity and charm are more closely associated with the Absolute in its highest expression than is majesty. And although it is seen that loving motivation is not lacking in his other *avatāras*, because of an excess of grandeur expressed there, love in its fullest expression is not their *līlā*.

Truth may be beauty, but beauty is also bewildering. Thus, truth is bewildering as well. Were it not so, it would not be beautiful. Such is Kṛṣṇa *līlā*, about which we are cautioned not to try to understand with our intellect alone.[35] The path of passionate love (*rāgānugā-bhakti*), by which one can realize the bewildering beauty of the truth of Rādhā-Kṛṣṇa, is dealt with in the concluding chapter of this book.

Is truth beauty? Before anyone ventures to answer, let them hear the *Śrīmad* (beautiful) *Bhāgavatam* (truth). Let them hear about Rādhā (*Śrīmad*) Kṛṣṇa (*Bhāgavata*) from the lips of the disciples of Śrī Caitanya, the Goswāmīs, and their followers. Doing so, they will know not only the "one word of truth that outweighs the entire world," but the whole truth of the beauty that will save the world from both the misery of sensuality and the emptiness of mere sensual restraint.

There is no more potent and profoundly beautiful section of the *Bhāgavatam* than the *rāsa-pañcādhyāya*. These five chapters relate the love dance of Rādhā-Kṛṣṇa and the gopīs. The *rāsa-pañcādhyāya* picks up just as Kṛṣṇa passes his tenth year. He has already done many miraculous things in the rural setting of Vraja along the banks of the Yamunā River. Many tantrics, assuming terrifying forms by their mystic prowess, have attempted to kill Kṛṣṇa. Without difficulty, Kṛṣṇa has slain them all, as devotion to him easily slays the many demons that linger within the heart of the spiritual aspirant. In spite of Kṛṣṇa's miraculous acts, however, the inhabitants of Vraja could not but think of him as their dearmost, according to whichever of the principal varieties of *bhakti-rasa* they live within. The fact that Kṛṣṇa performs miraculous acts is ordinary; the fact that God acts like a human is extraordinary. He does so because it is in human life that one can understand love. Human life is special, not merely because it comes with the power of reasoning, but more so because in human life one can realize one's potential for love. When both God and soul meet face to face in human life, love makes her appearance as well. Along with Kṛṣṇa comes Rādhā.

The gopīs' love, and Rādhā's love in particular, are exclusively featured in this section of the *Bhāgavatam*—the *rāsa-pañcādhyāya*. Rādhā is love, selfless and pure. She personifies that which brings God and humanity together to taste love. In doing so, she emerges bringing victory to Kṛṣṇa over Cupid, or *kāma* (lust).

Lust is that selfish desire that passes as love for as long as, and to the extent that, God is not present in the human equation. Kṛṣṇa is also known as *kāma*, but he is *kāmadeva*, the God of desire. Thus he conquers all desire, not by extinguishing it, but by redirecting it to himself. He does so through the agency of his primary *śakti*, Śrī Rādhā, *premamayī,* the abode of love.

Thus in the battle between Kṛṣṇa and Cupid that the *rāsa-pañcādhyāya* represents, *prema*, the highest love personified as Śrī Rādhā, is victorious; yet true to her nature, she gives the victory to Kṛṣṇa. If we enter the arena of the description of *rāsa-līlā* with lust in our hearts, we will come out with love alone.

Cupid no doubt reasoned that victory was assured for him. The playing field being the human form of life, where "the spirit is willing but the flesh is weak," must have appeared to Cupid to offer home field advantage. Moreover, he met Kṛṣṇa in the darkness of night, illumined only by the enchanting beams of the harvest moon. The surroundings were the beautiful forests of Vraja, full with night-blooming jasmine, and flowers and foliage of all descriptions. Cupid did not even bother to bring his soldiers, seeing that Kṛṣṇa was already surrounded by the most beautiful women in the universe, the gopīs. Nor did Kṛṣṇa resemble God in appearance. But much to his surprise, *anaṅga* (Cupid, who is invisible)[36] was defeated by Kṛṣṇa (*kāmadeva*). The spiritual *kāmadeva*, who establishes a relationship with the soul, defeats Cupid through the means of Cupid's own flower arrows (*puṣpabāṇa*) of form, taste, touch, smell, and sound. Govinda (Kṛṣṇa, who gives pleasure to the senses) engages the soul's senses in experiencing him, and thus establishes himself as the transcendental Cupid (*anaṅga*), with whom the soul can experience eternal love.[37]

The love of the gopīs that appears outwardly like lust is the secret of Vraja. It is never played out in the open. The very nature of the highest love is that it hides itself. It is so cleverly hidden in the guise of lust that even the *ṛṣis* often do not think to look for it within Kṛṣṇa *līlā*. The gopīs' love is hidden even from the other inhabitants of Vṛndāvana. Although a number of Vraja's eternal residents have direct knowledge of Kṛṣṇa and the gopīs' mutual love, they are careful to keep the secret, lest it be known publicly by all and be stripped of the veil that serves to enhance its experience. *Pārakīyā*, or paramour love, is not a partial expression of *mādhurya-bhakti-rasa*, but it is its fullest expression of conjugal love. This is the *bhakti-rasa* of the gopīs, amongst whom Śrī Rādhā is the dearmost of Kṛṣṇa. Although worldly paramour love is immoral, it nonetheless serves to illustrate the unbridled nature of love in its highest intensity. The highest aesthetic rapture of Rādhā-Kṛṣṇa is thus expressed in terms that are outside the bounds of secular aesthetics. In secular aesthetics, that which is immoral can never produce *rasa*, the experience of beauty. Yet we must remember that Rūpa Goswāmī has adjusted secular aesthetic theory to fit his Vedānta, revealing a theory of divine aesthetics in which Kṛṣṇa is the owner of all, the true husband of all souls. Thus, in *pārakīyā-madhurya-bhakti-rasa* there is no blemish. Rādhā's love for Kṛṣṇa is faultless.

To make Rādhā's greatness known, Candrāvalī gopī serves Kṛṣṇa as her competitor in the eternal drama. Thus there are two principal groups of gopīs in the *rāsa-pañcādhyāya*: those dear to Rādhā and those dear to Candrāvalī (there is also a third neutral group). Yet these other gopīs are all expansions of Rādhā herself, necessary in the drama so that its theme of love be relished comprehensively.[38] The script weaves a story of love with all its nuances, replete with passion, tenderness, jealousy, anger, union, and separation. Yet all such nuances, being Kṛṣṇa-centered, are expressions of *bhakti-rasa*, and thus have little in common with the lustful love that pervades human life devoid of God consciousness. True love never suffers from overexposure. Finite worldly love, by contrast, turns into aversion and thus cannot lead to that which all souls seek—infinite, eternal love.

A healthy distaste for self-centered material life is helpful for tasting and digesting the *rāsa-pañcādhyāya*.

However, theoretically it is not essential. Such is the spiritual power and purity of *rāsa-līlā*: By repeatedly hearing *rāsa-līlā* from a mature devotee of Kṛṣṇa, the vilest person can be converted into a votary of Mādhava.[39] With all of its symbolism, *rāsa-līlā* is like a heart swollen with a tale that escapes explanation. If we are fortunate to penetrate its philosophical message entwined in its story of love, and by the grace of *śrī-guru* fall in love with Kṛṣṇa, we too can live in the ideal world of Rādhā-Kṛṣṇa, the ultimate truth that is both beautiful and bewildering.

The English retelling of the *rāsa-pañcādhyāya* that follows leaves much to be desired, in that it or any attempt at translation could never convey the richness of the original Sanskrit language in terms of poetic and literary aesthetic content. No earthly language is as precise (truth) and romantic (beauty) as Sanskrit. Moreover, Sanskrit is equipped to convey concepts that have been all but lost in the march of materialistic modern and postmodern civilization. These sublime concepts have no corresponding words in English. Nonetheless, the rendering is faithful to the spirit of the text, and embellished with additional revelations of the

Goswāmīs, their contemporaries, including Śrī Vallabhācārya,[40] and their followers, including myself, in an unbroken chain from master to disciple extending over the last five hundred years.

CHAPTER TWO

Rāsa-līlā

Pray tell can sweetness be more sweet?
And then more sweet, a sweetness even more complete?
With just one drop the entire cosmos fills
and drowns within its lovely honey swills;
in sweetness all directions merge and meet.

The smiling rays of camphor touch his lips.
The smile melts from his misty mouth and drips
entering by force the ears of all the skies
it beguiles, and ravishing it ties
the hearts of all and, most of all, the girls.

Just hear about the dulcet flute's disgrace!
It steals wives from their husbands' sweet embrace,
destroys their dharma and their chaste vows.
And Lakṣmi too in heaven is aroused,
so what hope have we poor girls to save face?[1]

ALTHOUGH ŚRĪ KṚṢṆA is full in himself, the autumn nights scented with the fragrance of night-blooming jasmine stimulated him to enjoy his *līlā* of love. The taste for conjugal love that is inherent in his nature was thus allowed to manifest due to the autumn season.

Bharata's ancient doctrine of aesthetics lists the autumn nights as one of the *uddīpanas,* or stimuli, for conjugal love. Being the fountainhead of all existence[2] and the reservoir of aesthetic experience, Kṛṣṇa is the origin of the propensity for this love. When we speak of Kṛṣṇa, we speak of the very source of all being and experience described in the Upaniṣads. Kṛṣṇa is not the sectarian God of a few, but the Absolute, the ground of being, and more importantly the embodiment of the joy that all souls exist to taste.[3]

Kṛṣṇa's conjugal love is not touched by the material inebrieties that frustrate our expression of such love. His desire is a product of the necessity to celebrate his fullness,[4] not one resulting from the lack that we souls experience due to misidentifying with matter. To meet this desire, he activated his internal *śakti* and called the gopīs to dance with him in the dead of night.

Previously, he had promised the unmarried gopīs that he would meet with them and fulfill their desire to marry him by enjoying with them.[5] They had fasted and performed penances, petitioning goddess Kātyāyanī to give them Kṛṣṇa as their husband. They thus demonstrated that although they appeared to be mere village girls, their love for Kṛṣṇa constituted comprehensive and realized knowledge of the Vedas.

The worship they engaged in had both an exoteric and esoteric significance. Exoterically, the sacred Vedas encourage material enjoyment through the performance of ritual. Thus there are rituals for acquiring a good husband, good children, good health, and so on. However, the Vedas, seen in their esoteric light, prescribe only the pursuance of transcendental love. While the Vedas seem to encourage material prosperity through religious ritual, their deeper intent is to awaken faith in themselves.

When, through the execution of prescribed rituals, one acquires the desired material result, faith in the Vedas awakens. This faith is the true fruit of the ritual. As this faith develops in a person, he naturally looks more deeply within the Vedas, only to find their secret teaching. This secret teaching leads to liberation from material life and the development of love of God. This is the sole purpose of the Vedas.[6] The gopīs must have performed Vedic rituals in previous lives to have arrived at their particular approach to the Vedic rituals, through which they hoped to get the Absolute Truth personified as their husband.[7] So intense was their desire for loving God that it can only be compared to the love of a young woman for her lover. They performed the Vedic ritual prescribed for getting a good husband, yet the spirit of their observance was to have an intimate transcendental relationship with the Absolute, rather than to marry into a life of material illusion. It was this spiritual passion alone, and not the benediction of the goddess, that assured their success. The sincerity of their approach is evident from the fact that Kṛṣṇa accepted their proposal.

During the observance of their vows, while the gopīs were bathing in the Yamunā river, Kṛṣṇa had come and stolen their clothes. At that time, he had given the gopīs assurance that in the future he would embrace them in love. One year later, with the rising of the harvest moon, the autumn nights in the beautiful Vṛndāvana forest provided the most suitable setting in which to fulfill his promise.

As Kṛṣṇa's mind thus turned toward love, the full moon, king of the stars, rose on the eastern horizon. The reddish rays of the moon, who is the presiding deity of the mind, covered the sky and dispelled the suffering of those who watched him, just as a lover meeting his beloved alleviates her pain of separation.

This moon appeared to be the very mind of Kṛṣṇa, who would preside over the minds of the gopīs as the moon presides over all the stars. The moon's reddish rays revealed the passionate temperament of Kṛṣṇa as he contemplated the love dance he was about to engage in. The Upaniṣads also identify the moon with virility, and there is no better evidence for this than this evening when he who is the joy of the moon dynasty expressed his mind's desire to enjoy passionate love with the gopīs.

Rising in the east, the moon's sending its rays in all directions seemed to speak to Kṛṣṇa of paramour love. It was as if the moon spoke thus:

I am the moon, who brings happiness to everyone,
and I am the lover of the wives of the gods of the directions.
You too are 'the moon'; why do you now tarry
to make love, not going to the wives of other men?[8]

The east is the direction of the gods, and thus this passionate desire of Kṛṣṇa's is godly and free from impropriety. He is the *pūrṇa avatāra* and all belongs to him, and he will reveal such on this occasion, just as the moon reveals that the night belongs to him alone when he expresses himself in all his fullness. Kṛṣṇa's desire to enjoy love with the gopīs informs us of his fullness and proprietorship over all. It also sheds light on the darkness of false proprietorship that underlies the material experience.

When Kṛṣṇa saw his mind in the form of the passionate moon, the face of his beloved, Śrī Rādhā, appeared in the moon of his mind as well. It was as if the brilliance of her beauty appeared as the bright shine of the autumn moon. Kṛṣṇa also saw the *kumuda* lotuses blooming in response to the moon's beams as they shone upon the forest. Thus to the lotus of his lips he applied his flute, calling the gopīs and Śrī Rādhā to join him. Desiring *anurāga*, he played his musical *rāga* of love.[9]

By this time, Kṛṣṇa had perfected his flute playing, which was intended all along to attract Rādhā. Previously, he had met with only partial success. At first, he was successful in enchanting the various forest creatures. Later, he successfully attracted the other gopīs, but Rādhā fainted and did not come.[10] During the entire rainy season, Kṛṣṇa had practiced his flute playing, thinking that by so doing he could perhaps enhance the beauty of the autumn season, bringing it under his control by the time its full moon arrived. By doing so, he would be able to captivate Rādhā, who would be captivated by the autumn season itself. Indeed, this time he was successful, causing the fragrant *mallikā* flowers to bloom out of season and during the night rather than during the day.

The sound of the fifth note of Kṛṣṇa's flute, which expresses his passion, entered the ears of Rādhā and the gopīs and stole their hearts. Their passion, aroused already in their hearts due to the full face of the autumn moon, was thus increased, and they left their homes unbeknown to each other to capture the thief of love who had stolen their hearts. The gopīs each heard their own name in the sound of Kṛṣṇa's flute, and as they ran, their earrings swung to and fro in their haste.

Kṛṣṇa's flute has eight holes and thus eight notes by which he attracts all living beings. The fifth note is especially for the gopīs. It is said that the goddess Gāyatrī, the prototype of all Vedic mantras, heard that the personified Upaniṣads aspired to take birth as gopīs[11] and that they were successful. Desiring the same for herself, she appeared as *Gopāla-tāpanīya* Upaniṣad, in which the *kāma gāyatrī* is explained. The fifth note of Kṛṣṇa's flute is this same *kāma gāyatrī mantra*.

Some of the gopīs were milking cows when they heard Kṛṣṇa's flute, yet they stopped in the midst of milking and ran to Kṛṣṇa. Others left milk boiling on the stove, while still others left their baked goods in the oven. Some were dressing, others feeding children, others rendering service to their husbands. Still others were bathing, taking their meal, or applying cosmetics, but all of them stopped what they were doing and ran to Kṛṣṇa, even with their clothes and ornaments in disarray.[12]

In Vedic society, women were cared for in all stages of life so that they could be free to render their essential service to society without being burdened with the task of seeing to their own maintenance. The importance of womanhood, its chastity and motherhood, was understood in terms of its being vital to the health of society. Thus, as children, women were cared for by their fathers, as young women by their husbands, as widows by their sons and relatives. In this case, the gopīs were charmed by the only true protector of all souls. Having heard his flute calling them to unite with him in passionate love, they left the relative protection of socio-religiosity to enter the homeland of the soul.

In this world, all protectors are only relatively so. Although the importance of an ordered society is not to be underestimated, even when that order is aimed at leading all souls in the progressive march toward transcendence, the apparent transgression of socio-religious customs that sometimes occurs as a by-product of transcendental love can never be condemned. The gopīs, while appearing to transgress the socio-religious guidelines, had realized the goal of such guidelines.

Their passion was perfection because it was directed to the perfect object of love—Śrī Kṛṣṇa.

Another group of gopīs, however, could not escape the prison of their home life. They were gopīs who in their previous lives as the Upaniṣads personified had cultivated a transcendental relationship with Kṛṣṇa but had not yet achieved the perfection of that culture. Although they could not physically go to meet Kṛṣṇa, the fire of their separation from him burned away the last remaining traces of material influence in their consciousness.[13] Thus freed from karma, they attained transcendental bodies like those of Kṛṣṇa and the other gopīs. These gopīs then became qualified to associate with Kṛṣṇa directly on future nights.

Śrī Caitanya taught the doctrine of love in separation as a means of union with the Absolute. The yearning that is characteristic of separation from one's beloved is the intensity with which one must cultivate spiritual life. The group of gopīs who were checked from union with Kṛṣṇa exemplify this teaching.

Separation and union are two banks of the river of love. Separation serves to accent union, and union holds within itself the fear of future separation. Thus in the union of the gopīs with Kṛṣṇa, separation loomed. This eternal play of union and separation represents a dynamic concept of union much different from that of monistic Vedānta. As the union presented in the *Bhāgavata* is different from static monistic union, the concept of separation from Kṛṣṇa is different from the separation between lovers in the material world. In the material experience, although separation often makes the heart grow fonder, this is not always the case. Moreover, there is no material pain to transcendental separation. This is so because Kṛṣṇa *līlā* moves around the pleasure of Kṛṣṇa. Wherever he wants to go, his devotees are satisfied, for their only objective is his pleasure. Furthermore, the separation of the gopīs intensifies their devotion to him. When they feel transcendental suffering, it is because they know he cannot be fully happy without them.

Kṛṣṇa *līlā* can be seen as a metaphor for an ontological reality that human society can contemplate, and at the same time Kṛṣṇa *is* that ontological reality—the perfect object of love. As such, no matter how one fixes one's mind upon Kṛṣṇa, one will attain transcendence in due course. If it is possible for one to attain a transcendental result even by absorption in enmity toward Kṛṣṇa, what must be the result of one who becomes absorbed in passionate love for him?

Transcendence is a variegated experience, the apex of which is reached by absorbing the mind in the Absolute. In devotional Vedānta, absorbing the mind during meditation does not result in the object of meditation becoming more and more abstract until one ultimately reaches a formless reality. In other systems, the object of meditation is not important. In *bhakti*, however, the only object of meditation is the Deity—Kṛṣṇa. The result of meditating upon Kṛṣṇa is that one develops more and more devotion for him, until one actually experiences the direct vision of Kṛṣṇa and his *līlā* and ultimately enters there, never to return to the world of duality. The devotee, that is, enters a dynamic union in love with the Absolute wherein he realizes oneness *in purpose* with Kṛṣṇa.

Absorbing the mind in the Absolute is the goal of meditation, and since there is no more consuming mental state than that of passionate love, this passion for Kṛṣṇa is the realization of that goal. When this is cultivated within the context of spiritual practice, one can attain a spontaneous relationship with God similar to that of the gopīs. Although the gopīs seemed to merely lust for Kṛṣṇa, their eagerness for his association was a product of many lives of spiritual culture.

Seeing that the gopīs had arrived, Kṛṣṇa greeted them with charming but confusing words. He welcomed them with praise and asked what he could do for them. He first questioned them to determine if they had come to request a favor, indicating that if they had, they should simply ask and he would oblige them. Secondly, he queried about their hasty approach. Had they run into the forest because of some dreadful occurrence in the village?

From these first two inquiries, we learn that there are various motives with which people approach God. People sometimes approach God only for the purpose of gaining a blessing from him so that their family life will be improved. Others approach God out of frustration in social and familial affairs, rather than out of mature understanding of the positive value of spiritual culture. This second group rejects the world in pursuit of liberation. Kṛṣṇa thus inquired about the gopīs' motive for coming to him. If it was neither of the above, then Kṛṣṇa wanted to know, "Why did you come?" This final question indicates that there is a third motive for approaching God, a motive that can only be explained by way of claiming to have been "called." This is pure *bhakti*, in which the devotee has no motive (*ahaituki*). The devotee comes to Kṛṣṇa out of love. Such devotees desire neither material gain nor liberation from *saṁsāra*—they only want to love Kṛṣṇa. This is the best reason for approaching God, and it was no doubt the gopīs' mood. They came on his terms, answering to the clarion call of his enchanting flute. It was, although an invitation to all, heard only by a few.

Before the gopīs could say why they came, Kṛṣṇa teased the gopīs, testing their resolve. He warned them of the dangers of the night, both its darkness and its inhabitants.

> *"The dreadful night is quite frightening,*
> *and so its creatures too,*
> *return home slender-waisted,*
> *this is no place for girls like you."*

Kṛṣṇa's words confused them, for they could be taken in two ways. Overtly, he seemed to be encouraging them to go home. However, covertly he was encouraging them to stay. On the surface, Kṛṣṇa warned them of the danger of the night, which even though well-lit due to the full moon's rays, was dangerous because of wild animals. Furthermore, they were in danger of moral degradation, for they were alone at night with a young man. He cautioned the gopīs about the nature of the mind in such circumstances, for men and women together are like butter and fire.

Yet covertly, through the exercise of indirect speech, Kṛṣṇa was encouraging the gopīs to remain with him. Kṛṣṇa had called the gopīs, and he was not merely testing them. Although fully God, he was also fully human.[14] Thus his speech was invested with dual meaning. As God, he felt it necessary to give them a final warning of what they were about to do. As their lover, he desired union with them.

While Kṛṣṇa seemed to be saying "don't stay" (*vrajaṁ neha stheyam*), his actual intention was to say "don't go" (*vrajaṁ na, iha stheyam*). Regarding the fearful night with its dangerous animals, Kṛṣṇa indirectly told the gopīs that the night was not at all fearful for them, because its darkness and ferocious animals would keep their husbands and family members away. Thus he told them to stay with him and not go home. They would be safe with him, for the forest would protect them from anyone who might come after them. Regarding the potential for moral degradation that the circumstances seemed to lend themselves to, Kṛṣṇa told the gopīs that because he was a *brahmacārī*[15] and they were chaste ladies, there was no cause for concern.

Kṛṣṇa continued to confound the gopīs by telling them that their mothers, fathers, sons,[16] brothers, and husbands, not seeing *(apaśyantaḥ)* them were searching for them in a panic. Yet in warning them thus, he secretly told them that these family members would not find them, in case the gopīs feared that the place of their meeting was not safe. If the mothers gave up, their fathers would come. If they failed, the gopīs' sons and brothers would come. If they too failed, their husbands would come with even greater determination, but none of these relatives would find them. At this point, the gopīs were truly lost—lost and found.

Hearing Kṛṣṇa's speech, the gopīs began to look around at the beauty of the forest night. They did not dare to look him in the eye for fear that what he seemed to state was his actual intention. Scanning the forest's moonlit beauty, they looked everywhere but at him. Kṛṣṇa, seeing their reaction, told them, "Now you have seen the forest with its flowers shining in the light of the full moon, and you have seen the beautiful trees with their leaves trembling in the cool breeze coming from the Yamunā. Therefore, do not delay here any longer, go home *(tad yāta mā ciraṁ goṣṭham)*, serve your husbands and feed the crying babies."

Kṛṣṇa addressed the gopīs as *satī,* or chaste, as indeed they were, for everything belongs to Kṛṣṇa, and they were acknowledging this by surrendering themselves to him. Yet outwardly he told those gopīs who were already married—Rādhārāṇī, Lalitā, Viśākhā, and others—that they had a reputation to uphold and religious duties to perform in conjunction with their husbands, and should therefore return home. He told the unmarried gopīs that they should tend to the needs of the calves, and the gopīs who were married to return to their husbands and village children and feed them.

The flowers were in bloom, but their fruits were yet to come. Reddened by the moonlight, the flowers suggested that this was the perfect time for love. By mentioning the fullness of the moon, Kṛṣṇa indicated that where there is fullness one should stay. Those who have only partial devotion, clinging still to the world of illusion, can never be full and thus never stay with him. The evening breeze was cool and favorable. All of these signs of nature indicated that the gopīs should delay, and not go for some time *(tad yāta mā, ciraṁ goṣṭham)*. Regarding their children and calves, Kṛṣṇa indicated that those interested in happiness should not go where there is suffering.

Kṛṣṇa then told the gopīs, "Perhaps you have come here out of great love for me, compelled by this alone. This, of course, is laudable, for all living beings love me." All living beings may not love God directly and acknowledge his proprietorship, but they all love that which he alone provides. Kṛṣṇa told the gopīs that if love was their motive, it was proper. However, even in stating this, Kṛṣṇa continued to speak indirectly, for it is not artful to engage in direct speech, and thus he appeared to continue to encourage the gopīs to return home. Kṛṣṇa told the gopīs that they did not understand how to properly execute devotional life. There was no need for them to stay there with him, rather they should continue to execute their religious duties toward husband, family, and children even while cultivating their love for God. Thus Kṛṣṇa preached to them regarding the worship of God. Yet this kind of worship of God is not the kind of love the gopīs had for Kṛṣṇa.

Thus Kṛṣṇa differentiated here between the gopīs' love for him and the love all other living entities feel toward him. He described the gopīs' love as *yantritāśayāḥ*, with hearts subjugated, compelled by love, while he described the love all other living beings feel as general affection, *prīyante mayī.* Thus he indicated that the gopīs must stay with him.

In telling the gopīs that it is a woman's duty to serve her husband, Kṛṣṇa was also instructing them to stay with him, for he alone is the real husband. Kṛṣṇa said that the wife should serve her husband without duplicity. Yet the word *amāyayā* also means without illusion. To serve the husband (*bhartuḥ*, the protector) without illusion is to serve Kṛṣṇa.

Kṛṣṇa continued, "Women who desire a better life in the future should never abandon a husband, even if he is of bad character, unfortunate, old, stupid, sick, or poor, as long as he is not fallen." Here Kṛṣṇa indicates that because he has six opulences in full,[17] as long as a person has devotion to him, even if such a person has the six faults mentioned or worse, he is to be considered saintly. Such is the value of devotion to Kṛṣṇa, by which one eventually develops all the good qualities of the gods. If a person has no devotion to Kṛṣṇa, however, he has little, even if he has all good qualities.[18]

Kṛṣṇa then condemned adultery, stating that such acts bar one from higher planets in the next life and ruin one's reputation in this life. Furthermore, adulterous acts are accompanied by fear and performed only with difficulty. Thus he makes it clear that what he is actually proposing regarding their meeting is not what it appears to be on the surface. The meeting of Kṛṣṇa and the gopīs is transcendental to both pious and impious acts.

Concluding his speech, Kṛṣṇa told the gopīs that transcendental love for him is not dependent upon physical proximity. It grows out of directives found in sacred literature that recommend hearing about Kṛṣṇa, seeing his form in the temple, meditating upon him, and chanting his glories. Kṛṣṇa anticipated that the gopīs might respond to his suggestions about chastity by differentiating between their love for him and ordinary love. Thus he pointed out to them the scriptural path of regulated ritualistic devotion (*vaidhi-bhakti*), in which the notion of passionate love for God does not arise. There is, however, another path, that of spontaneous devotion (*rāgānuga-bhakti*). It was this path that the gopīs had chosen, and entering Kṛṣṇa's circle of intimate love is the goal that the gopīs realized. On the *rāga-mārga*, the devotee adheres to scriptural injunctions, performing devotional activities such as hearing, chanting, viewing the temple deity, and meditation, yet with a motive to enter the circle of intimate, and even passionate, transcendental love. This was the gopīs' chosen path, one that should not be misconstrued to advocate mere physical proximity to Kṛṣṇa.

The gopīs heard what Kṛṣṇa said to them, but they assumed that he was rejecting them. They thought that their desires were contrary to Kṛṣṇa's will and thus felt embarrassed and dejected, their dreams shattered. They looked to the ground as if it were about to swallow them. Their breathing became heavy and their lips parched. With their toes they scribbled in the dust, and the tears from their eyes washed away their mascara and mixed with the saffron they had smeared on their breasts.[19] Standing in silence, their grief knew no bounds. Yet they noticed that Kṛṣṇa too had become silent. They had forsaken everything for him. They had withdrawn their passion for every other person or thing, yet he had spoken to them as if he were another person, not the one who a year ago had accepted their proposal for amorous love. His apparent rejection, however, did not affect their love in the slightest. This again is a symptom of real devotion, as is the fact that their passion for Kṛṣṇa involved the loss of passion or desire for anything else. They were not about to turn back, even at the formidable obstacle presented by Kṛṣṇa's apparent rejection and orders to return home. Thus they collected themselves and with faltering voices[20] began to speak. They stammered in their speech, both because they were upset and because they were about to oppose the orders of the Absolute Truth personified.

The spirit of the gopīs' reply is instructive. They were justified in challenging what Kṛṣṇa seemed to say, for it was not at all proper for him to reject such surrendered souls. His words of apparent rejection were not in concordance with the spirit of the sacred texts. When the sacred literature seems to say something that is in contradiction to its own conclusions, we must seek a deeper meaning in those words. The words of the sacred texts must be taken seriously, but their inner meaning must be ascertained if we are to benefit from them. Often persons cite a text but do not understand its spirit. To be angered by so-called scriptural speech that is divorced from the spirit of sacred literature is a sign of devotion.

The gopīs accused Kṛṣṇa of speaking to them cruelly, for although he initially seemed to welcome them *(svāgatam)*, he was not at all accommodating. Nor was it proper for him to have asked them about the situation in their village, for he knew well that to come to him they had abandoned the village without a thought. For Kṛṣṇa to insist that they return home was contradictory to the innumerable statements of sacred literature that assure us that his realm, arrived at through devotion and love, is the land of no return. They insisted that he accept *(bhajasva)* their love, just as Viṣṇu accepts the love of his devotees, even though they desired a transcendental relationship with him of greater intimacy than one based on the awe and reverence that Viṣṇu's devotees have for their Lord. Although the gopīs approached Kṛṣṇa with an apparently erotic intent, their feelings were in fact of a religious and spiritual nature, their lover being the original person.[21]

The gopīs then told Kṛṣṇa that his instructing them on religious principles, in which he is the ultimate authority, was appropriate. Indeed, women should serve their husbands and relatives. In stating this, the gopīs implied that with regard to religious duty *(dharma)*, two things must be considered: *dharma* must be learned and it must be executed. In order to execute religious principles, one must learn about them from a guru. The guru and his service are thus the basis of *dharma*. Kṛṣṇa was speaking correctly about *dharma* as an expert guru, and the gopīs stated that as such he should be worshipped first and foremost. Without worshipping him, how could they properly perform their religious duties, or even know about them?

Understanding the basis of religious life is more important than mindless execution of religious principles. Furthermore, the religious duties pertain for the most part to one's body, and only indirectly to one's soul. Successful execution of religious ritual, however, should culminate in an interest in the soul. Thus one who through religious ritual and duty develops interest in the soul and the supreme soul truly executes *dharma*. The gopīs, being interested in the fullest expression of *dharma*, saw fit to neglect their bodily obligations and tend to the needs of their soul and the service of the supreme soul, who is the *pati,* or husband and maintainer, of all souls.[22] Thus the gopīs disagreed with Kṛṣṇa by way of agreeing with him, giving their own purport to his words. Their speech was gentle and loving, addressing him as *preṣṭha*, "dearest one," as they countered his arguments.

The gopīs continued, "The wise find pleasure in loving you, who are their very self. In comparison, what are husbands and relatives who are sources of suffering for the soul? Therefore, O Lord who bestows blessings, be merciful to us, and do not knowingly cut asunder our ardent and long-cherished desire to love you."

The gopīs indicate in this statement that wise persons agree with them that service to Kṛṣṇa is true happiness. *Dharma* must have as its goal a pleasurable end in order for one to be motivated to execute it. The wise who know this understand *dharma* to be service to the inner self, which in a qualitative sense is one with God. Conversely, wise persons conclude that service to family members cannot be the *dharma* of the self, for it leads only to suffering by way of perpetuating *saṁsāra*. Service to family members cannot be *dharma* because it does not truly have a pleasurable result as its goal. If service to family members constituted true *dharma*, there would be no *saṁsāra*.

While the gopīs cite the wise to give support to their argument, they say something to the wise as well. The wise who tread the path of knowledge identify themselves with God, and God loves them as his very self.[23] But there is another class of devotees whom he loves *more* than his self. They are not satisfied with knowledge of their qualitative oneness with the Absolute. They are not content to know God eternally. They desire to serve him actively in transcendence, and in the case of the gopīs, to love him passionately. Such love constitutes the fullest expression of *dharma*.

The gopīs' long cherished hope to exchange love with Kṛṣṇa kept them alive and attentive to family affairs. Should this hope go unfulfilled, there would be no meaning to their returning to their families. If their hopes to love Kṛṣṇa were cut asunder, their ties to relatives would cease to exist as well.

The gopīs continued, "Our chance to be engaged in family affairs has been stolen by you, who have captured our minds, hands, and feet, which will not move a step from here. How then can we return to our village, and if we somehow did, what would we do there? You ask if we have come to see the forest, but without our minds what will we see? Effortlessly you have stolen our minds, and thus it was easy for you to steal everything else we owned as well. Because you are joy itself standing before us, no other means of attaining joy holds any attraction for us.

"The path of knowledge *(jñāna)* requires a strong mind and intelligence, but we do not have these. Religious duty on the path of action (karma) and other means of attaining joy are meaningless in your direct presence, for not only has our power of thinking been stolen, but our power to act independently of you has been stolen as well. You have stolen our hands that otherwise might be doing housework. Without hands how can we act? Our hands are impassioned to touch only you.

"When you told us that we have already seen the forest and therefore we should return home, you did not consider that our feet are now rooted like trees in you alone. As trees cannot move independently of their roots, so we cannot move from your presence. If you suggest that we now go back by some other means, again, what would we do there in this condition?

"O dearest one, Kṛṣṇa, please pour like a flood the nectar of your lips onto the fire of our hearts, which has been stoked by your smiling glance and soothing song. If you refuse to do so, dear friend, we will consign our bodies to the fire of separation and travel by meditation the path tread by your lotus feet. If you truly want us to go, we will go quickly by that fire of separation. Therefore, you should continue to give life to the fire of desire in our hearts, which you yourself have created. This fire of *kāma* dies with the death of the body. Only you can keep *kāma* alive by accepting our desire for you, for you alone are the eternal love. Without (*vi*) giving us your passionate love (*raha*), we will burn without it in separation (*viraha*). Without (*vi*) your love *(raha)* we will remain in solitude *(viraha)*, and without solitude with you, our desire for love *(kāma)* will not have any life. In this way we will die and thus attain you."

Referring to Kṛṣṇa's statement about their having come to him out of love, the gopīs replied that this was indeed the case. Thus they began to speak about the nature of that love. It was such that merely upon seeing his footprints they lost all interest in anyone else. The same feet whose touch is cherished by the goddess of fortune, Lakṣmī,[24] tread throughout the Vṛndāvana forest, giving joy to its inhabitants and stealing the hearts of the gopīs. Referring to Kṛṣṇa as the Lord of the forest dwellers, the gopīs imply that he truly loves those who have given up everything for him, for the sages dwell ever in the forest.

The gopīs compared their love for Kṛṣṇa to Lakṣmī's love for Nārāyaṇa, for it was predicted at the time of Kṛṣṇa's birth by Gargamuni, the family astrologer, that Kṛṣṇa would be like Nārāyaṇa himself.[25] As Nārāyaṇa gives shelter to his devotees, the gopīs suggested that Kṛṣṇa should give them shelter. Should the chastity of their love be contrasted with that of Lakṣmī, the archetype of the faithful wife whose first love was Nārāyaṇa, the gopīs pointed out that Lakṣmī too wanted to leave Nārāyaṇa's chest to get the dust of the feet of Kṛṣṇa. Lakṣmī sought the dust of the lotus feet of Kṛṣṇa in fear of losing her fidelity to one of the many who courted her favor, for once having attained the footdust of Kṛṣṇa, one can never be captured by anyone else. Thus the gopīs indicated the transcendental superiority of Kṛṣṇa over Nārāyaṇa and the appropriateness of their seeking the shelter of his feet. As he granted this opportunity to Lakṣmī, so also should he grant it to them. They came to the forest out of love for him alone and requested that he decorate their fair bodies with the jewels of his dark blue limbs.

The gopīs asked Kṛṣṇa to bestow upon them the benediction of becoming his slaves (*dehi dāsyam*). They did not think that divine slavery was merely an act of offering oneself. Service is not the prerogative of the servant, but rather a gracious grant from above. Thus they approached him not as ordinary women with passion for love, but in a divine passion, which transcends the material notions of woman and man.

They addressed Kṛṣṇa as the destroyer of sins, indicating that in approaching him they could not be guilty of any sin themselves.[26] They requested that he accept their refutation of his words and bless them, for they were eligible for his mercy, having left their home life behind.

The gopīs continued, "Seeing your face framed by the curls of your hair, your cheeks beautified by earrings, your beautiful lips like a pool of nectar smiling between your cheeks, your strong arms that dispel our fear, and your chest that is the residence of the goddess of fortune, there is no alternative for us other than to enlist as your maidservants."

Earlier, Kṛṣṇa had instructed the gopīs that abandoning one's husband brought degradation both in this life and in the next, ruining a woman's chances for liberation. Why then should the gopīs choose to be his slaves, rather than ask for liberation? Anticipating that Kṛṣṇa might reply to their request for divine slavery by suggesting that various types of liberation are available for those who worship him, the gopīs restated their request answering this objection: They said that the mere vision of Kṛṣṇa's smiling face makes the desire for liberation disappear. The prospect of tasting his lips lies not in liberation but in *prema*, divine love, which is full of various tastes *(rasas)* relished by both Kṛṣṇa and his devotees.

The fear of the gopīs arises from the possibility of repercussions for their actions. Yet because of Kṛṣṇa's strong arms they are fearless. If their husbands should complain to Kaṁsa, the king of Mathurā, still they have nothing to fear. It is through his arms that Viṣṇu accepts the sacrificial offering of the gods, who seek his protection from the demoniac. If by his arms he can protect Indra, the king of heaven, certainly he can protect them from their human husbands. Furthermore, should Kṛṣṇa attempt to counter their request by questioning the morality involved in his embracing them, the gopīs reminded him that his chest is the resting place for the goddess of fortune and thus the residence of the highest *dharma*. This is so because good fortune results from *dharma* alone. It is on this chest that they wanted to rest from the night.

"Dear Kṛṣṇa, what woman throughout the universe would not be distracted from ordinary religious life by the sweet melody of your flute? Your beauty makes everything auspicious. Even cows, birds, trees, and deer exhibit symptoms of ecstasy, their hairs standing on end upon seeing your form. You have appeared on earth primarily to remove the anxiety of your devotees here in Vraja. You may do other things as well, but those things can be done through your incarnations. Protection of the inhabitants of Vraja is not the work of any of these incarnations. It is your job, and you should perform it dutifully, just as Nārāyāṇa protects his servitors in his abode. Therefore, friend of the distressed, in the highest expression of *dharma*, please place your hand on our breasts and heads."

Thus, through their words in despondence, the gopīs demonstrated their love, and Kṛṣṇa, the master of all mysticism, smiled at them. Showing them his mercy, he began to enjoy with them, even though he was self-satisfied. In the assembly of the gopīs, infallible Kṛṣṇa appeared like the moon amidst the stars. The magnanimous Kṛṣṇa caused the gopīs' faces to blossom through his glances, as his smiling teeth shined like jasmine flowers. Then Kṛṣṇa sang in praise of the autumn moon and the beauty of the lily ponds, while the gopīs repeatedly sang a refrain consisting of Kṛṣṇa's names alone.

doing so, he also gave the gopīs the opportunity to experience love for him in separation, for the learned Bharata has explained in his *Nāṭya-śāstra* of aesthetics that union is not fully appreciated until separation has been experienced.

THE SEARCH

When Kṛṣṇa suddenly disappeared, the gopīs were grieved at loosing sight of him. They appeared like a group of female elephants who had lost their mate. The lover they had lost could be compared to only a bull elephant, about which the *Kāma-sūtra* informs, "Only the bull elephant knows fully the delight of love." Having experienced such a lover and suddenly lost him, the gopīs' separation knew no bounds.

In this sorrow of separation, the gopīs found Kṛṣṇa within themselves, remembering his gestures and deeply affectionate smiles. They remembered his playful glances, his words, and his various pastimes with them. Full of affectionate attachment, their minds became entranced with thoughts of he who is the master of beauty, and thus they began to enact Kṛṣṇa's pastimes themselves. Indeed, they began to imitate his bodily movements, smiling, affectionate glances, speech, and other features. Maddened by remembering Kṛṣṇa's pastimes, when some gopīs asked where he was, others declared themselves to be him.

The gopīs' madness in love caused them to adopt their lover's mind, sending theirs to him. As the *Kāmasūtra* instructs us, when a woman's love becomes too great, she becomes like a man. So also the gopīs, embracing Kṛṣṇa's mind, naturally assumed his bodily movements, for the body follows the mind. Whatever we contemplate, the body is sure to follow in due course.

Although some of the gopīs declared themselves to be Kṛṣṇa, they began searching for him at the same time. Thus they simultaneously experienced their qualitative oneness with the Absolute and their quantitative difference. They did not actually become Kṛṣṇa, for if they had there would have been no further possibility for *rasa* with him. Thus their feelings of oneness with him are described using the word *vibhramāḥ*, mistaken. Theirs was a case of mistaken identity caused by love. Moreover, *vibhramāḥ* also means beauty. Thus this was merely a beautiful pastime, *vibhrama-vilāsa* of the lover and his beloved.[28]

Both the followers of Rādhā and Candrāvalī gathered together in one group and wandered throughout the forest, singing loudly as if insane.[29] As they moved about, they asked the trees as to the whereabouts of Kṛṣṇa, who like space is within and without all things. Thus, through the description of *bhakti* flowing from the pen of Vyāsa and the mouth of Śukadeva, the gopīs instruct us in two important ways as to the means of spiritual progress: the efficacy of spiritual song and good company.

The gopīs sang loudly and in unison. Joining together in song in praise of God, *kīrtana*, has been highly recommended by Śrī Caitanya and his disciples. *Kīrtana*'s marginal characteristic is that it quickly cleanses the heart and affords liberation from birth and death. Its primary characteristic, however, is that it awakens the soul to the aesthetic experience *(rasa)* of Kṛṣṇa in devotional love.

This chanting can be strengthened by the company of those who are spiritually advanced and by the good advice found in such company. The gopīs thus inquired from the trees who are the *vanaspatiḥ*, or lords of the forest. They are so because of their benevolent nature in providing shade and shelter, as well as an abundance of nourishment for all who dwell there. The trees not only give all these things, but they do so without being asked. The trees are paradigms for ideal human behavior, that which is exemplified by the Vaiṣṇavas, the devotees of Viṣṇu. From the Vaiṣṇavas, we can get good advice, and thus strengthen our resolve and deepen our understanding of the efficacy of all acts of devotion. We can learn the way to find he who is everywhere. We can learn, that is, to find ourselves, our relationship with the center—Kṛṣṇa—for it is we alone who are lost. "More humble than a blade of grass, more tolerant than a tree, when will my mind attain these qualities?" With this frame of mind the true Vaiṣṇava searches for Kṛṣṇa, and thus stands like a tree of the forest of life, showing us the way.

The gopīs first approached the three worshippable trees: pippal, fig, and banyan. These trees are identified with the Hindu trinity: Viṣṇu (pippal), Brahmā (fig), and Śiva (banyan). The gopīs reasoned that surely these trees would know the location of their lover, who had stolen their hearts with his love, smiles, and glances. Because these trees refused to speak, the gopīs thought they should further identify who they were looking for. Therefore, they referred to Kṛṣṇa as "the son of Nanda," as young wives in Hindu culture usually do not refer to their husband by first name. Identifying him as such also served to explain their plight. Someone had stolen their hearts. Neither Viṣṇu nor any of his incarnations steal, but Kṛṣṇa, the son of Nanda, certainly does. He steals, however, that which belongs to himself, for the gopīs' hearts, touched by his charming *līlā*, could never belong to anyone else.

When the pippal, fig, and banyan remained silent, the gopīs approached other smaller flower-bearing trees. "O red amarantha, aśoka, nāga, punnāga, and campaka! Has the younger brother of Balarāma [Kṛṣṇa], whose smile destroys the pride of conceited women, passed here?" The gopīs reasoned that these trees had more sense of love, for flowers are always involved with loving affairs, and thus they would surely respond to their need.

When these trees also remained silent, the gopīs turned to the holy basil, tulasī, for unlike the other trees who lent themselves to many uses, tulasī was exclusively dedicated to the worship of Kṛṣṇa. Furthermore, unlike the other trees, tulasī was female and thus surely she could sympathize more with a young lady's love. They addressed her with respect, "O auspicious one, O tulasī who holds the feet of Govinda very dear, have you seen he who is infallible walk by, wearing a garland of your flowers, encircled by swarms of fragrance-hunting bees?" But tulasī did not reply. The gopīs concluded that because tulasī is always used in the worship of Kṛṣṇa, she is both proud of her position and knows nothing of love in separation. How then could she sympathize with them? Furthermore, why would she? Like any wife, she guarded her position and did not care to give it up to another.

Turning from the silent tulasī, the gopīs spoke to the four common varieties of jasmine creepers: "O malatī, O mallikā, O jātī, O yūthikā, has Spring himself, Mādhava, passed you and pleased you by his touch?" Yet they too did not reply.

The gopīs then turned to the fruit-bearing trees, such as the most magnanimous mango, which lined the banks of the Yamunā. These were the Vaiṣṇava trees, which stood like immortal sages along the sacred river's eternal flow. The mango in particular lives only for others. Thus the gopīs said, "Please tell us, who have been deprived of our very selves, which way Kṛṣṇa has gone." Because they conceived of these trees as Vaiṣṇavas, the gopīs did not hesitate to refer to their lover by his foremost name Kṛṣṇa, for this name, more than any other, would capture the attention of his devotees. They pleaded the peculiarity of their case, for they had lost not their house or home, but their very selves. It is the self that the Vaiṣṇavas are concerned with, and that in terms of its relationship with Kṛṣṇa.

Receiving no reply from the trees, the gopīs concluded that perhaps they were in *samādhi*; thus, they turned their attention to the earth. Thinking themselves most unfortunate, they praised the earth, for she was constantly being touched by Kṛṣṇa's lotus feet. They saw the trees as her hairs, which were standing in ecstasy due to Kṛṣṇa's touch. "O earth, what austerities did you perform to attain the good fortune of being touched by Keśava's lotus feet? This has brought you such joy that your hairs are standing on end, and thus you appear very beautiful."

The gopīs too had performed austerities to get Kṛṣṇa as their husband, and thus had constant access to his feet. But they considered themselves unsuccessful in comparison with the earth. Therefore, they questioned the earth, "What type of austerities did you perform? What was the nature of your *sādhana*?" Not only was the earth blessed by Kṛṣṇa's feet, she was blessed in previous millennia by his incarnations: Vāmana and Varāha. The gopīs further inquired from the earth as to just when her ecstatic life began. Was it when Vāmana's stride covered the earth's surface or, more likely, when Varāha embraced her?[30] Or was it due to the present circumstances?

The gopīs in Rādhā's camp, headed by Lalitā, then turned to the doe and inquired from them. Certainly they would be sympathetic, for although they had husbands, their true love was also Kṛṣṇa. "Wife of the deer, dear friend, has Acyuta passed by here with his beloved, striding with long legs and widening your eyes with joy? In this place the breeze brings the fragrance of his jasmine garland mixed with the saffron of his chosen lover's breast."

Rādhā's group knew well by now that Kṛṣṇa was with her alone, while Candrāvalī's group remained unaware or still unwilling to admit this. Thus Rādhā's group refers to her here. Rādhā's group wanted to catch up to the divine couple, for they knew Rādhā and Kṛṣṇa's loving exchanges would be enhanced in their company, expert as they were in arranging their loving affairs.

When the deer did not answer, the gopīs concluded that they could not speak about Kṛṣṇa in front of their husbands. As the deer moved deeper into the forest, they stopped and glanced back at them, and the gopīs thought that they must be indicating for them to follow. Surely, then, they knew where Kṛṣṇa was. When they lost sight of the deer, the gopīs thought that they were hiding themselves because finally Kṛṣṇa was nearby.

The gopīs then noticed a group of trees bent over and assumed they had just paid respect to Kṛṣṇa. They turned to them and inquired as to his whereabouts. "O trees, seeing your bowed position, we can understand that the younger brother of Balarāma, his left hand on the shoulder of Rādhā, his right carrying a lotus, has passed here. He must have been followed by swarms of intoxicated bees, who were chasing his garland of tulasī flowers. Did he acknowledge your homage with a glance of affection?"

The silent sage-like trees were perhaps unwilling to talk to mere village girls, and thus the gopīs addressed their wives, the creepers, who embraced the trees. These creepers never offered the flower of their true love to their husbands, even though appearing to embrace them. The gopīs thus surmised that surely they too were familiar with paramour love and would understand their plight. "Let us ask the creepers about him. Although they are embracing their husbands, it is clear that they have been touched by Kṛṣṇa's fingertips, for the constant embrace of one's husband does not produce the kind of horripilation we see on their bodies." The gopīs thought that Kṛṣṇa must have touched these creepers and picked their flower offering, which he had in turn given to Śrī Rādhā. If so, surely the creepers, of all the forest inhabitants, would sympathize with Rādhā's group, for like them these creepers had turned from their trees/husbands for assisting Rādhā in her love with Kṛṣṇa.

The gopīs' maddened manner of speech, in which they spoke to the trees, the earth, and the deer is instructive. The gopīs had deep spiritual love for Kṛṣṇa. One of the primary symptoms of one who has this deep transcendental love is that she thinks she has no love. It is said *ātmavan manyate jagat*, "In this world, one thinks others to be like oneself." In this way, the gopīs thought that the trees, earth, and deer had more devotion than themselves. The world became alive with emotion for Kṛṣṇa. They saw everything in light of their own love for him. While the neophyte on the devotional path often thinks that he is a true devotee while others are not, the mature devotee feels that all others are serving Kṛṣṇa, save and except for himself. As one approaches the Absolute, one's finite nature in relation to the infinite is felt. Thus the closer one comes to the infinite, the further from it one feels, for such is the nature of the infinite, whose presence is humbling, yet reassuring.

After being unsuccessful in their questioning the various flora and fauna, the gopīs began to feel discouraged in their search. They then entered into a deep devotional trance in which they began to imitate the various pastimes of Kṛṣṇa. One gopī imitated the witch Pūtanā, who had attempted to kill Kṛṣṇa by offering him her breast smeared with poison. Another imitated Kṛṣṇa's killing of Śakaṭāsura, who had assumed the form of a cart in an attempt to take Kṛṣṇa's life. Another gopī imitated the whirlwind demon Tṛnāvarta, while another, imitating Kṛṣṇa, pretended to kill the demon. Another gopī imitated Kṛṣṇa's infancy by crawling about. Two gopīs imitated Kṛṣṇa and Balarāma, while others played the parts of cowherd boys. One pair of gopīs imitated Kṛṣṇa and his killing of Vatsāsura, and another pair, Kṛṣṇa's killing of Bakāsura. When another gopī imitated Kṛṣṇa calling his cows by playing on his flute, others congratulated her, exclaiming, "Well done! Well done!" Still another gopī imitated Kṛṣṇa by putting her arm around a friend announcing, "I am Kṛṣṇa. Just see how gracefully I move!" "Don't be afraid of the wind and rain," said another as she lifted her shawl above her head, imitating Kṛṣṇa lifting Govardhana Hill. One gopī climbed on the shoulder of another and stepped on her head imitating Kṛṣṇa chastising the serpent Kāliya. She shouted, "Get out of here, you evil snake. I have taken birth to punish creatures like you!" Another gopī exclaimed, "Hey cowherds, quickly close your eyes and I will protect you from this raging forest fire." Then one gopī imitated mother Yaśodā binding Kṛṣṇa, whose part was played by a friend. In doing so, she used a flower garland, pretending it was a rope as she put it around the slender waist of her friend. As she did so, her friend covered her face as if terrified.[31]

With the pastime of mother Yaśodā tying Kṛṣṇa, the gopīs' imitative games ceased. Significantly, they ended their imitation of his pastimes with one in which he was tied up, conquered by love. In all of this imitation, the gopīs' *sthāyī-bhāva,* or permanent emotion of love, as Kṛṣṇa's paramours was never interrupted. All that is pleasurable in any of the other flavors of *bhakti-rasa* is also present in *parakīya-rasa,* or paramour love. Thus without aesthetic conflict (*rasābhāsa*), they continued to experience *parakīya-bhāva* in *mādhurya-bhakti-rasa,* even while imitating a variety of Kṛṣṇa's pastimes.

While the gopīs were thus entranced, they suddenly came to external consciousness and noticed Kṛṣṇa's footprints. "These footprints clearly belong to the great soul who is the son of Nanda, for they are marked with a flag, lotus flower, thunderbolt, *cakra,* elephant goad, barleycorn, and other signs." The flag on Kṛṣṇa's foot symbolizes the assurance that his devotees will live without fear. The lotus flower increases his devotees' eagerness for him, for their minds are just like honeybees. The thunderbolt symbolizes Kṛṣṇa's ability to cut down mountains of inauspicious karma for those who take shelter of him. The *cakra* stands for his protective nature. The elephant goad symbolizes Kṛṣṇa's ability to conquer the elephant of one's mind, and the barleycorn indicates that his devotees will be famous. These are only some of the auspicious and uncommon marks on the bottom of Kṛṣṇa's right foot. The gopīs saw both of his footprints and followed them into the night. Becoming weary as they searched, they all realized Kṛṣṇa was not alone for his footprints were accompanied by those of another gopī. Seeing this, Candrāvalī's group of gopīs became somewhat disheartened.

Analyzing the pair of footprints, the gopīs reached various conclusions. "Here we see the footprints of a gopī who must have been walking alongside the son of Nanda. He seems to have been resting his forearm on her shoulder, just as an elephant rests his trunk on the shoulder of his mate." The gopīs of Candrāvalī's group thought that perhaps the gopī had spirited Kṛṣṇa away from their dance. On the other hand, because they had seen only the footprints of Kṛṣṇa, they suddenly realized that it was possible he had been carrying her, and that it was he who had stolen her from the scene of the *rāsa-maṇḍala*. At any rate, they were obviously very intimate, for their footprints indicated that they were walking off-balance.

Then Candrāvalī, her pride diminished, admitted, "Certainly this gopī is well named as Rādhā, for she has perfectly worshipped Govinda, who is full of the all-attractive opulence of sweetness and thus controls all by stealing their hearts. He was so pleased by her that he abandoned all of us and brought her to a secluded place. O girls! Even Brahmā, Śiva, and the goddess of fortune take Govinda's feet upon their heads in an act of consecration, yet here we see that these feet themselves have become purified by association with the feet of Śrī Rādhā. It appears that it is she who is worshipped by Govinda."

Lalitā, Śrī Rādhā's confidante, in order to tease Candrāvalī then said, "The fact that Rādhā's footprints are alongside of Kṛṣṇa's does indeed prove that he has selected her and is now alone with her. Though this is nothing to be remorseful over, the fact that she is now tasting the nectar of his lips may indeed be something for you to lament about."

Viśākhā gopī, another of Rādhā's dearmost, studying the footprints in greater detail, said, "Look, here Śrī Rādhā's footprints are no longer present with Kṛṣṇa's. Surely her tender feet must have been troubled by the grass and thus her lover picked her up and carried her."

Candrāvalī gopī added, "Look, here Kṛṣṇa's footprints sink deeper into the ground due to Rādhā's weight. He must have had difficulty carrying her. He is so lusty that he has ignored our love and gone with Rādhā, and over here that intelligent boy must have put her down in order to pick flowers."

Rādhā's younger sister, Anaṅga Mañjarī then said, "Just see how Kṛṣṇa must have collected flowers for Rādhā here. Only the impressions of his toes are visible where he reached for the flowers."

Then Śrī Rūpa Mañjarī added, "Here Kṛṣṇa must have put those flowers in Rādhā's hair, anointing her as the queen of Vṛndāvana's forest."[32]

Thus Kṛṣṇa took pleasure in none other than his own soul, Śrī Rādhā, and in doing so revealed the shallowness of male lovers and the hard-heartedness of their female counterparts. Worldly lovers do not love at all, unaware as they are of their own selves. Kṛṣṇa revealed this through extolling Śrī Rādhā's love above all others'. Although outwardly Śrī Rādhā appeared to be selfish in wanting to have Kṛṣṇa to herself, the truth of her heart is selfless love. Such is the nature of *prema*, the highest spiritual love. *Prema* is so pure and confidential that it hides itself in the guise of lust just to keep those possessed of lust from plundering her.

As the gopīs proceeded in madness through the forest, they discussed the pastimes of Rādhā and Kṛṣṇa. At that time, Śrī Rādhā, Kṛṣṇa's love for her now confirmed, felt remorse for the other gopīs who were suffering in separation. She knew that she alone could fully satisfy Kṛṣṇa, and only because of this had she put herself first. If any of the other gopīs could have pleased him more, she would have been the first to push that gopī forward. Yet now she felt for her friends in their hour of need. She knew well the pangs of separation herself, and thus she devised a plan to mitigate the suffering of her friends. Outwardly showing pride,[33] she told Kṛṣṇa that she could walk no farther and asked him to carry her. Speaking thus, she attempted to slow Kṛṣṇa's pace so that the other gopīs could reach them.

Although fully satisfied in her company alone, Kṛṣṇa understood the softness of Śrī Rādhā's heart and the selfless nature of her love. Thus he desired to further demonstrate the nature of that love to the other gopīs. Kṛṣṇa reasoned that if the gopīs were to come upon the two of them, they would not know fully the glory of her love. However, if they were to see her in a moment of separation, the intensity of that separation in contrast to their own would reveal that the depth of her love was greater than all of theirs combined. While thinking thus, Kṛṣṇa suggested that Rādhā climb on his shoulders. At this thought, her love swelled to the height of *mahā-bhāva*.[34] In that ecstasy, Rādhā could not see Kṛṣṇa, and she thought he had disappeared. Śrī Rādhā in the intensity of her love in union thus simultaneously experienced intense separation. Witnessing that separation, even Kṛṣṇa himself was astounded by her symptoms.

Śrī Rādhā cried out for Kṛṣṇa, the great connoisseur of *rasa*. "Where are you, my love? The full blossom of my youth is for you alone. You were so charmed by me that you left all the other young and beautiful gopīs and took me alone with you. You can do as you like with me as it suits your passion; however, I will surely die in this separation. This thought is giving me pain, for without me, as you have already demonstrated, you will not be happy."

Seeing the *sāttvika bhāvas* of Rādhā, Kṛṣṇa experienced more than ever the glory of her love. Yet, just at that moment, he noticed the other gopīs approaching and he hid in the bushes. As Kṛṣṇa watched, the gopīs consoled Śrī Rādhā, overwhelmed by the intensity of her love. Seeing her condition, the gopīs described her thus:

> *Is this the golden campaka vine which has fallen here,*
> *or is it the silver of the moon,*
> *or the tutelary deity of golden light,*
> *or the incarnate beauty of the Vṛndāvana forest?*
> *Alas! How terrible! She is not moving, why?*[35]

Their minds filled with anxiety for Rādhā, the other gopīs all swarmed around her like bees around a flower garden. Both her friends and competitors then fell unconscious. Although Rādhā's body was permeated by Kṛṣṇa's scent, when she smelled the additional fragrance of Kṛṣṇa coming from the other gopī's bodies, she returned to external consciousness. Identical in consciouness with their mistress, Rādhā's friends awakened along with her.

Comforting Rādhā and seeking to enlighten those ambivalent to her, Rādhā's friends asked why Kṛṣṇa left her. Rādhā then instructed them as to the external cause of Kṛṣṇa's disappearance from the *rāsa-maṇḍala*. Declaring him faultless, she attributed his disappearance to her own pride. Such was her humility.[36]

Then, with her guidance, they all began to search for Kṛṣṇa. They entered deep within the forest where even the moonlight did not shine. Śrī Rādhā suggested that if Kṛṣṇa was not interested in meeting them at this time, their chasing after him would force him to go deeper within the forest without the light of the moon and thus cause him inconvenience. Thus she suggested that they go to the banks of the Yamunā and sing together in praise of him, longing for his return.

SONGS OF THE GOPĪS

Forlorn in knowing that Kṛṣṇa could not be happy without them, and especially without Rādhā, the gopīs gathered together and sang about him. The gopīs sang out of separation from Kṛṣṇa, and in doing so they demonstrated the efficacy of *kīrtana*, or song in praise of God, for by their chanting they caused Kṛṣṇa to reappear in their midst.

Their song was full of humility, knowing from Rādhā the fault of their apparent pride. Such humility was advocated by Śrī Caitanya in his famous *Śikṣāṣṭaka*. Therein, in the spirit of Rādhā, he advised that one chant the name of God with more humility than a blade of grass. When one steps on a blade of grass, it never complains or shows resistance. With this disposition we can experience the efficacy of chanting the name and glory of God.

The gopīs sang thus:

> *"This land of Vraja is victorious over all, because you have taken birth here. Because of your birth in Vraja, the goddess of fortune takes refuge here. O beloved, we who are purchased by you look for you in all directions. Please reveal yourself to us!"*

The gopīs began their songs by praising Vraja itself, the plane of the highest love. Its victory over all other places is complete, for even Lakṣmī, the goddess of fortune, took refuge in Vraja. Nārāyaṇa's consort left him to seek out Kṛṣṇa, and so doing, took shelter in Vraja. There, this great goddess eternally waits in line to have union with Kṛṣṇa. One can thus imagine the exalted position of the gopīs, who won Kṛṣṇa's embrace every night.

Everyone wants the blessings of the goddess of fortune, and they perform great austerities to get her company. Yet she lives in Vraja where she performs austerities in an effort to attract the attention of Kṛṣṇa. It is said that the goddess of fortune was unsuccessful because she wanted him on her terms and failed to follow in the footsteps of the Vraja-gopīs, treading the secret path of passionate love.

The goddess of fortune is an expansion of Rādhā, as are all the consorts of Kṛṣṇa's innumerable incarnations. Thus Vraja is also glorious because this Goddess of ultimate good fortune, Śrī Rādhā, lives there perpetually. Only by her grace can one enter there.

The gopīs looked for Kṛṣṇa in all directions, yet in doing so they never left Vraja. Vraja is the best of all places, and sacred literature tells us that Kṛṣṇa never leaves Vraja. This is so because he is conquered by the love of its inhabitants. What is a place but its inhabitants? Thus the gopīs indirectly extolled the virtue of their own love, the very essence of Vraja, which belittles the love of Lakṣmī for Nārāyaṇa.

Vraja indicates a pasturing ground. Historically, Vraja was not a fixed place, for the cowherds moved as required for the sake of their livelihood, their cows. Kṛṣṇa is known as Govinda, he who gives pleasure to the cows, and thus his abode moves out of his love for his devotees and their love for him. From this, we can understand something about the nature of eternal Vraja, the land of transcendental love. It is not fixed and static, but dynamic in its eternal flow. It is roaming in search of the Absolute, with a passion like that of the Vraja gopīs. Vraja is that place which harmonizes all. Even the passion of the gopīs finds its perfection in Vraja, where "all things are completely appropriate."[37]

The gopīs continued:

> *"O Lord of love, with your eyes you steal away the beauty of autumn's best lotuses, as they bloom within the ponds. If you do not look upon us now with those same eyes,*

verily you will kill us, who have committed ourselves to you in slavery. Is this not murder?"

Big thieves are often murderers as well, and the gopīs accuse Kṛṣṇa of murder herein, for he is no small thief. The autumn-lotus is well-protected by its surrounding waters, and moreover it blossoms during the day when all are present to see. Thus stealing its beauty is not possible for anyone other than a very big thief. The gopīs claim that they are living for his glance, but if he does not bestow it, how will they go on living? They had offered themselves with no expectation of reward other than his association, yet he did not even look upon them.

The lotus is the symbol of beauty, and the autumn lotus is especially beautiful. Here the gopīs compare its beauty to that of Śrī, the goddess of fortune. As Kṛṣṇa's eyes steal away the beauty of the goddess of fortune, those upon whom he bestows his glance are truly beautiful. Such is the gopīs' aspiration, that they might be beautified by the glance of the God of love. He is such, *surata-nātha*, and unless he expresses that love with them, who will know of him as the God of love? For the sake of his own reputation, they implore him to cast his glance upon them and continue with his *līlā* of love.

> *"O bull among men, you saved our settlement from so many dangers, such as poisoned drinking water, a man-eating serpent, wind and rain, lightning and fire, Māyā's son (Vyomāsura), and other types of difficulties from all directions."*

Here the gopīs refer to various calamities that occurred in Vraja, reminding Kṛṣṇa of how he protected them at those times. All of the incidents occurred previously,[38] and the gopīs are remembering them as the exploits of their protector. From such remembrances, one can gain confidence in taking shelter of Kṛṣṇa. Many demons lie within our hearts and prevent us from progressing spiritually. The incidents describing Kṛṣṇa's slaying of demons referred to by the gopīs can be meditated on to destroy the practitioner's inner demons. Each of the demons who caused difficulty to the inhabitants of Vraja exemplifies a particular *anartha*, or impediment to entering the spiritual life of Vraja. Only when these *anarthas* are eradicated can one enter the *rāsa-līlā*. Thus the gopīs instruct us as to the prerequisite for participating in Kṛṣṇa's highest love sport. Furthermore, they inform us that Kṛṣṇa is the ultimate male, a bull among men who will destroy all misgivings within our hearts. It would be fruitless to take up another path to first cleanse the heart, and then proceed to approach Kṛṣṇa with passionate love as our ideal, for no one is more capable of cleansing our hearts than him, and his demon-killing *līlās* attest to this in no small measure. He is the bull, *ṛṣabha,* and by extension, the husband or protector *(bhartṛ)* of all who surrender to him. Should he not then protect the gopīs in their death of separation?

> *"Although others know you as the indwelling guide of all, are you not the son of Yaśodā? Asked by Brahmā to descend on earth, O friend, you took birth in the dynasty of the Sāttvatas."*

Singing thus, the gopīs reveal that they are aware of all aspects of Kṛṣṇa's divinity, yet they are more concerned with that which pertains to their own lives, the fact that he is the son of Yaśodā. Worship of Kṛṣṇa in passionate love includes the worship of all forms of God and all types of transcendental love.

Kṛṣṇa is the indwelling guide, and he responded to Brahmā's appeal at a time when the earth was overburdened by the mentality of exploitation. He responded to the human/earthly plight, because he is at home in human society, and Vraja on earth is his homeland. Although Kṛṣṇa is *sāttvatām kule*, born of the Yadu dynasty, he is the son of Yaśodā first and foremost, for her parental love exceeds all others, and Kṛṣṇa is controlled by his devotees' love.[39]

The indwelling guide, Paramātmā, is neutral. He witnesses all and interferes with no one. But this is not so with Kṛṣṇa. He may also be the indwelling guide of all in his partial manifestation as Paramātmā, but the gopīs know him as the son of Yaśodā, and as such, he should be partial to their plight, for they are also objects of Yaśodā's love.

While the Paramātmā feature of God is characterized by impartiality, the Bhagavān feature is ornamented by partiality toward his devotees. Ordinarily, partiality is a defect, especially in relation to spiritual life. God, it is thought, must be impartial. As the indwelling guide he is impartial, but as Kṛṣṇa he is partial to those who love him, an opportunity open to all. It is partiality devoid of ignorance that fuels the spiritual world. It is the partiality of *bhāva*, spiritual emotion, that manifests only after one has crossed beyond the world of friends and enemies. The gopīs are devotees of this caliber, and thus Kṛṣṇa should reappear before them, for they know him on intimate terms, as the son of Yaśodā.

Furthermore, if Kṛṣṇa appeared on earth at the request of Brahmā for the protection of the pious, certainly the gopīs should not be ignored, for piety lies in satisfying God, and at this they were most expert. Moreover, Kṛṣṇa should appear before the gopīs even in consideration of the fact that he is the indwelling guide, for they have not ignored his guidance like others. They have followed him everywhere, as he follows all, residing in their hearts.

> *"Greatest of the Vṛṣṇis, place your reassuring lotus hand on our heads. We have come to you driven by aversion to saṁsāra. Your hand instills fearlessness in persons like us and stirs passion, as in the case of the goddess of fortune, who has taken your hand in marriage [in your form of Nārāyaṇa]."*

Although the gopīs understand Kṛṣṇa to be the greatest of the Vṛṣṇis, they desire that he place his cooling lotus hand on their heads. The fact of his greatness does not diminish their desire for intimacy, as it might others who realize their object of love to be such a great person.[40] The nature of their love is so strong that even knowledge of Kṛṣṇa's supremacy does not interfere with their perception of him as their lover. As a mother who learns that her son has been elected president continues to think of him first and foremost as her son, the gopīs continue to think of Kṛṣṇa as their lover in spite of his other qualifications.

The gopīs inform Kṛṣṇa that they have come to him out of fear of *saṁsāra*. In this case, they refer to the home life that they left in order to be in his presence. They are confident that his cooling lotus hand will have a twofold effect. It will cool the fire of *saṁsāra* and stimulate the fire of passionate love within their hearts. Why is this so? He has already stirred such passion in the heart of the goddess of fortune, when as Nārāyaṇa he took her hand in marriage. Why then can't he similarly place his hand on their heads in affection, when he has already accepted them as his wives?

The gopīs continued:

> *"O you who vanquish the suffering of Vraja's people! Hero of women, your smile alone destroys the pride of the women of Vraja! O friend, everyone knows we are your servants. Accept us and show us the festival of your lotus face!"*

Here the gopīs reason that Kṛṣṇa appeared on earth to destroy the suffering of the people of Vraja in particular, for Kṛṣṇa is moved primarily out of love for his devotees. All other causes for his appearance are apparent only. Of all his devotees, the gopīs suffer the most. This is so because their love for him is filled with the separation of a paramour relationship. They cannot meet with him openly like his other devotees in Vraja. Thus their claim is well-founded.

Kṛṣṇa is the hero of all women, for he is the original expert in the art of love. The gopīs insist, should Kṛṣṇa not desire to reappear before them, thinking them to be proud, he need only smile at them and their pride will be vanquished. Pride is a mental attribute, but Kṛṣṇa's beautiful lotus face steals away the mind and thus removes the ground of pride.

A lotus appears on the water. In this case, Kṛṣṇa's lotus-like face appears on the nectar waters of immortality, and no one can drink the beauty of the nectar of immortality and remain faulty. If Kṛṣṇa does not believe them, the gopīs demand, "Then come and see for yourself. Show your lotus face!"

> *"Your lotus feet destroy the sins of those who surrender to them, they assist you in your cowherding, and they are the dwelling place of the goddess of fortune. You placed those feet on the head of the serpent Kāliya, so now please place them on our breasts and sever us from the pain of our hearts desire."*

Kṛṣṇa's feet are the abode of good fortune and the resting place of merit, conquering over all evil. In his appearance as Nārāyaṇa, the goddess of fortune, who is the emblem of piety, is eternally engaged in massaging them. But Kṛṣṇa roams the pasturing grounds and forests of Vraja, and he trounced the head of the serpent Kāliya, the personification of vanity. Certainly his soles must be coarse from this kind of activity in comparison to Nārāyaṇa's. Yet the gopīs suggest that Kṛṣṇa place those feet on their soft breasts, revealing just how soft the soles of his lotus feet are and how purifying they must be. The gopīs knew that the hard-hearted serpent Kāliya was softened by the touch of Kṛṣṇa's feet, as would their hearts, just beneath their breasts and contracted in separation, be relaxed by the same touch.

The *kāma,* or passionate desire, of the gopīs is their inner wealth. Yet they have submitted utterly unto Kṛṣṇa, and thus ask him to plunder that wealth with acts that appear impious, such as placing his feet on their breasts. Giving up one's wealth, one leaves the path of religion and pious works (*karma-mārga*) and enters a life of spiritual knowledge and asceticism. Yet the gopīs offer their wealth to Kṛṣṇa while remaining in what appeared to be bodily identification. Thus they tread neither the path of karma nor that of knowledge. Theirs is the path of passionate love, in which one transcends the formless Absolute, acquiring a spiritual form suitable for *līlā*. As Kṛṣṇa's feet follow the cows, who cannot listen to discourses on eternity, the gopīs insist that those feet also tend to their desire, for they cannot hear about how what they are doing might be irreligious, potentially barring them from eternity.

Unconcerned with anything other than his love, the gopīs sought the touch of his hand, his smile, his feet, and then the nectar of his lips and the sound of his sweet voice. His speech is so captivating, and he speaks in all languages. He is conversant in even the languages of the creatures, for in the least all creatures seek love and speak of it as best they can. No one knows this better than the gopīs; thus they asked to hear his voice and taste the sweetness of his lips.

> *"O lotus-eyed one, your sweet voice and charming words, which delight the minds of the wise, are bewildering to us. We are your maidservants. Please, dear hero, fill us with the nectar of your lips."*

While the wise delight in the philosophical ramifications of Kṛṣṇa's speech, the worldly are bewildered by them. What then is the position of the gopīs? Are they like the fallen souls who find Kṛṣṇa's speech bewildering? No, their bewilderment is of a different nature than that of even the gods and goddesses,[41] who cannot understand his speech.

The gopīs attraction for Kṛṣṇa's charming words is without concern for their philosophical ramifications, and thus they live beyond knowledge, or in the highest knowledge that mandates love. To know Kṛṣṇa in truth is to love him.[42] They delight not in the philosophical ramifications of his words, but in the words themselves. Their bewilderment is not the ignorance of common people. It is an expression of their love. They are bewildered about the divinity of Kṛṣṇa, not because their love is misdirected to another, but because it is so completely reposed in him. Such love causes the Absolute to appear to them, not as God, but as their lover.

Whoever broadcasts the words of and about Kṛṣṇa is the dearmost friend of all. Those who sing the glory of Kṛṣṇa thus came to the minds of the gopīs, as did the very virtue of such song itself.

> *"The immortal beverage of your words and the narration of your activities are the very life of those who suffer in material existence. Such narrations, distributed by poetic sages, eradicate one's* karma *and bestow auspiciousness upon those who hear them. These narrations are most beautiful, and being endowed with spiritual power, they flood the world. Those who recite them are the most charitable of all."*

That which the gopīs prayed for previously, Kṛṣṇa's reappearance, was appropriate, for they were indeed his devotees. Thus the gopīs thought that perhaps Kṛṣṇa had not returned because he did not consider them devotees. Had they been his devotees, how could they have continued living in his absence? Thinking in this way, they uttered this verse in praise of song about Kṛṣṇa and its bearers.

The gopīs' notion of what it means to be Kṛṣṇa's devotees is instructive. It informs us of the very measure of their devotion. In their mood, Śrī Caitanya prayed, "Not even the scent of love of Kṛṣṇa can be found in me, for had I such love, how could I continue to maintain my life in his absence?" This is the spirit of the gopīs' song. They answer their own conjecture as to Kṛṣṇa's reason for not reappearing. They tell Kṛṣṇa, "We are not concerned with maintaining our lives, but song about you keeps us alive anyway, for it is the nectar of immortality. It consists of the feeling and essence of the Absolute. It is *rasa* itself."

When we bring song about Kṛṣṇa into our lives, we get life. Outside of such spiritual culture, our "lives" consist of little more than the maintenance of a dead body, for it is the self that lives, not the body. If the self dies, it occurs not with the death of the body, but when the self identifies itself with the body, for the self is full and the body is empty. When we identify our self with the body, we feel incomplete, our existence threatened. We try to make our body enduring and beautiful only because we are so in our pure state, free from bodily and mental identification. If death of the self is bodily identification, life of the self begins with the death of the body. This is not physical death, but death to physical and psychic identification. Outside of this ego death, we continue to die again and again. Thus ego death is the end of the illusion of death and the beginning of life for the soul. As Hegel said, we must "die to live." For the gopīs, hearing and singing about Kṛṣṇa is the soul's life in transcendence, and one engaged in such song forgets to eat, sleep, mate, or defend.

Such is the virtue of *hari-kīrtana*, song about Kṛṣṇa. It is the life of the suffering soul, it quenches the thirst of the parched (*tapta-jīvanam*), and it frees the bound soul from its karmic embodiment (*kalmaśāpaham*). It is *rasa* itself and complete with the six opulences of

Godhead: wealth, strength, beauty, reputation, knowledge, and renunciation. What then can be said about those who sing this song to the world?

Although the gopīs lived on song about Kṛṣṇa, and thus maintained their lives in his absence, their lives are not free from disturbance. Explaining this, they continued to sing:

> *"O lover, your cheerful laughter, sweet glances, and captivating movements are all auspicious for meditation, yet they disturb our minds. Further, when you graze your cows, we think of the pain your feet might experience from the rough grass and pebbles, and that pain is transferred to our minds."*

The gopīs suggest that Kṛṣṇa is the perfect object of meditation. If he is the Absolute, then certainly this is so. Yet even if the object of meditation is arbitrary, as some meditative disciplines suggest, Kṛṣṇa's form may still be the perfect object of meditation. The reason for this is that it is easier to fix one's mind upon the beautiful person of Kṛṣṇa than any other object. The purpose of meditation is to still the movement of the mind. If Kṛṣṇa is the object of one's meditation, however, the mind can move as it is accustomed from his lotus feet to his charming smile, from his sweet words to his *līlā*, and so on. Yet while moving thus in meditation upon Kṛṣṇa's form, the mind remains still and undisturbed.

Kṛṣṇa roams the forest at daybreak, herding his cows with his friends. While so doing, he does not wear shoes. More certainly, he does not wear shoes made from the hide of those he loves so dearly, his cows. Kṛṣṇa's cows love him like a mother loves her son, and thus they are always eager to offer their milk to him. Kṛṣṇa is known as Govinda, or he who gives pleasure to the cows. When herding them he goes barefoot, for such is the tradition of the cowherders. When he leaves his house in the morning, his mother expresses a concern simular to that of the gopīs regarding the tender soles of Kṛṣṇa's lotus-like feet. At that time, Kṛṣṇa replies to her thus: "Mother, you don't know the forest path! I feel no trouble in tending the cows at all. It is my greatest pleasure! The paths don't give me any pain, for the Camarī deer sweep them with their tails, the trees shower them with their honey, and the Nabhī deer scent them with their navel musk! These paths are flawless and as soft as cotton!" Here, however, the gopīs are concerned that he may wander from the path, and the rough terrain may hurt his tender feet. The concern for Kṛṣṇa's potential pain is not a philosophical concern; it is the way of passionate love.

The gopīs continued:

> *"As the day dissolves, you return home. O hero, every time you display your face like a forest lotus, soiled by the dust raised from the hooves of your cows and covered by locks of black hair, you arouse passionate love in our minds."*

Here the gopīs sing of Kṛṣṇa's evening *līlā*, his returning from the forest with the cows. This time of day arouses passion in all.

Seeing that it is time to return and remembering his gopīs and their passionate love for him, Kṛṣṇa calls all of his 108 groups of cows, chanting their names on a rosary of jewels. His cows are grouped according to color. The 4 basic colors are white, red, black, and yellow, each of which have 25 subdivisions, making a total of 100 colors. Eight other groups consist of cows colored like sandalwood pulp, cows that are speckled, and cows with heads shaped like a *mṛdaṅga* drum, lion's heads, or other shapes, bringing the total to 108. The gopīs remember Kṛṣṇa with his cows, who beautify his face with the dust raised from their hooves. The word *rajas* means dust, as it does passion, for passion in normal circumstances covers the beauty of the soul. Yet here it is divine passion that is aroused in the minds of the gopīs upon seeing Kṛṣṇa's dust-covered, forest-lotus face. The gopīs indicate that their passion for Kṛṣṇa will be satisfied only by meeting him in the forest. He looks at them again and again as he returns, but he cannot meet with them at that time. Thus their passion is aroused but not satisfied in the village setting.

The gopīs then praised Kṛṣṇa's feet:

> *"O lover, your lotus feet fulfill all desires for those who bow before them. They are venerable for the lotus-born Brahmā, they decorate the earth, they are appropriate for meditation, and they represent the essence of peace. O destroyer of anxiety, please place them on our breasts."*

Although Kṛṣṇa's feet possess these qualities, only one who humbles himself and bows before them can realize this truth. Here the gopīs enumerate the positive qualities of Kṛṣṇa's lotus feet, whereas previously they had emphasized their power for removing inauspiciousness.

Then the gopīs praised the nectar of Kṛṣṇa's lips again in terms of their positive qualities.

> *"O hero, bestow upon us the nectar of your lips, which are kissed by your melodious flute. Those lips increase the lover's excitement and destroy sorrow, making people forget their attachments."*

Śrī Caitanya, while meditating on *rāsa-līlā* in the ecstasy of the gopīs, has described Kṛṣṇa's lips and flute thus: "His lips agitate the mind and body of everyone, they destroy the burden of material happiness and lamentation, and they make one forget all material tastes. The whole world falls under their control. They vanquish shame, religion, and patience, especially in women. Indeed, they inspire madness in the minds of all women. His lips increase the greed of the tongue and thus attract it.

"My dear Kṛṣṇa, since You are a male, it is not very extraordinary that the attraction of your lips can disturb the minds of women. However, I am ashamed to say this, but your lips sometimes attract even your flute, who is male.

"Aside from conscious living beings, even unconscious matter is sometimes made conscious by your lips. Therefore, your lips are great magicians. Although your flute is nothing but dry wood, your lips make it drink their nectar. They create a mind and senses in the dry wooden flute and give it transcendental bliss.

"That flute advertises its qualities and says to the gopīs, 'O gopīs, if you are so proud of being women, come forward and enjoy your property—the nectar of Kṛṣṇa's lips. Give up your shame, fear, and religion and come drink the lips of Kṛṣṇa. On that condition, I shall give up my attachment for them. If you do not give up your shame and fear, however, I shall continuously drink the nectar of Kṛṣṇa's lips.'

"This flute is nothing but a dry stick of bamboo, but it becomes our master and insults us in so many ways that it forces us into a predicament. What can we do but tolerate it? The mother of a thief cannot cry aloud for justice when the thief is punished. Therefore, we simply remain silent.

"What auspicious activities must the flute have performed to enjoy the nectar of Kṛṣṇa's lips independently and leave only a taste for the gopīs for whom that nectar is actually meant. The forefathers of the flute, the bamboo trees, shed tears of pleasure. His mother, the river, on whose bank the bamboo was born, feels jubilation, and therefore her blooming lotus flowers are standing in ecstasy.

"Consider how many pious activities this flute performed in his past life. We do not know what places of pilgrimage he visited, what austerities he performed, or what perfect mantra he chanted.

"Although the nectar of Kṛṣṇa's lips is the absolute property of the gopīs, the flute, which is just an insignificant stick, is forcibly drinking that nectar and loudly inviting the gopīs to drink it also. Just imagine the strength of the flute's austerities and good fortune. Even great devotees drink the nectar of Kṛṣṇa's lips after the flute has done so.

"The trees on the bank of the Yamunā and Gaṅgā are always jubilant. They appear to be smiling with their flowers and shedding tears in the form of flowing honey. Just as the forefathers of a Vaiṣṇava son or grandson feel transcendental bliss, the trees feel blissful because the flute is a member of their family.

"The flute is completely unfit for his position. We want to know what kind of austerities the flute executed, so that we also may perform the same austerities. Although the flute is unfit, he is drinking the nectar of Kṛṣṇa's lips. Seeing this, we qualified gopīs are dying of unhappiness."[43]

> *"When you roam the forest during the day, even a split second spent without seeing you seems to us like a millennium. Furthermore, when you return and we see your beautiful face and curly locks, we consider the creator, who made eyes that blink, a fool."*

Here the gopīs curse the creator, Brahmā. He is not their God. What is his fault? Eyes are meant to see beautiful forms. Yet, he created eyes that blink and thus cannot take full advantage of supreme beauty. Ultimately, it is not because we have eyes that we can see. Rather, our material eyes obscure our vision, for it is we who are the seers, not our eyes. Limited by our five senses and mind, we are unable to experience the limit of the truth that is beauty. The gopīs instruct us in this regard, yet more so as to the extent of their love. Who, when viewing an object of beauty, notices the blinking of the eyes? Such is the beauty of Kṛṣṇa, and such is the gopīs' perception of that beauty.

It is said that the gods of heaven do not blink, yet they cannot see Kṛṣṇa in their midst, for he appears on earth. If they see him, it is without blinking, and thus they see him in awe. He is earth's God, humanity's God, and human eyes blink. Because of this fault of human eyes, the gopīs saw Kṛṣṇa not as God, but as one of their own kind. Yet because they noticed the fault of their eyes, we can understand that they were neither human nor merely godly, but of the nature of Kṛṣṇa himself.

The gopīs continued:

> *"O infallible one, you know why we have come here, for nothing is unknown to you. We are enchanted by the song of your flute and have abandoned our husbands, other's children, ancestors, brothers, and other relatives. Who but a cheater like you would abandon young women like us who have come to see you in the middle of the night?"*

The gopīs tell Kṛṣṇa that although he is infallible, he is also a cheater, for having invited them, he refuses to shelter them. And now more than ever they require his shelter, for they have abandoned everything, including religious principles, to come to him in the night. How can one be infallible, reliable in all circumstances, and be a cheater, unreliable, at the same time? Such is Kṛṣṇa, in whom all contradictions are resolved.

Then the gopīs remembered Kṛṣṇa's confidential talks with them and sang thus, concluding their songs:

So soft and noble are your lotus feet.
We place them slowly on our breasts,
too rough, we fear, to give them any rest.
Do rocks and twigs not cause them pain
as they tread the Vraja forest's coarse terrain?
Our minds reel when we think thus of your feet,
for in you alone our lives are made complete.[44]

In this final verse, the utterly selfless nature of the gopīs' love is underscored, when appearing in a setting so conducive to and suggestive of selfishness. The contrast between love and lust is striking. The gopīs' desire to place Kṛṣṇa's feet on their breasts appears very much like lust. Yet the gopīs, although requesting

Kṛṣṇa to touch their breasts with the soles of his feet, desire him to do so only because it is the softest thing they possess. Pained by the thought of Kṛṣṇa's tender feet being pricked by the forest terrain, they are simultaneously pained at the thought of how rough their breasts are in comparison to Kṛṣṇa's lotus feet. Only for lack of something softer do they offer their breasts, not to enjoy him through their senses, but to please his senses.

REUNION

Having spoken incoherently while in search of Kṛṣṇa, and then expressing their hearts to him in song, the gopīs began to weep loudly, hankering for Kṛṣṇa to return. When the intensity of their plight of separation reached the point of extreme hankering, only then did Kṛṣṇa reappear.

Spiritual life is characterized by an absence of hankering,[45] for hankering is symptomatic of those who are unfulfilled. What then is the hankering of the gopīs? It is the full blossom of the flower of love, desireless desire. Hankering for Kṛṣṇa is realized when one hankers for nothing other than the highest truth, when one cannot live another moment without true love. This hankering is said to be the only price for the soul's union in love with Kṛṣṇa.

> *That heart absorbed in* Kṛṣṇa *rasa so rare—*
> *O friend, if you can find that rasa anywhere*
> *be quick to buy, how much the soul's in need!*
> *In that bazaar there's posted just one price;*
> *millions of pious works will not suffice,*
> *the only cost is paid in coins of greed.*[46]

Drawn by the gopīs' crying, Kṛṣṇa reappeared in their midst. Still drowning in their tears, the gopīs did not see him immediately. Garlanded and wrapped in a yellow cloth, Kṛṣṇa appeared as he who enchants the mind of Cupid. Kṛṣṇa smiled as if to say that his disappearance was all in jest. Yet realizing the gopīs' desperation, he wrapped his cloth around his neck in a gesture of humility for having hidden himself from those who were so deserving of his love. How could he hide from them any longer once their love had expressed itself so intensely? Their love was so divine that it necessitated the appearance of the God of love for its repose.

When the gopīs realized that Kṛṣṇa had reappeared, at first they thought they were hallucinating. When they realized they were not, they stood up, their eyes opening wide. As the rivers of the gopīs' tears dried, the flood of Kṛṣṇa's beauty, accented by his lightning aura, entered their eyes. His sudden appearance caused them all to come to life and stand to receive him. Had anyone else come, even a respectable person, they would have remained still and lifeless, for Kṛṣṇa alone was their very soul. Without him, they had no life, no love. Now that they had regained their life, their eyes opened wide, indicating their inner passion.

One gopī named Bhadrā repeatedly chanted the name of Kṛṣṇa in her excitement, and Candrāvalī clasped Kṛṣṇa's hand. Śyāmalā, standing on Kṛṣṇa's left, placed his arm anointed with sandalwood on her shoulder. A slender, delicate gopī named Śaibyā took the betel nut Kṛṣṇa had chewed, and Padmā, burning with love's desire, placed Kṛṣṇa's right foot on her breast.

With the exception of Bhadrā and Śyāmalā, all of the gopīs who surrounded Kṛṣṇa thought of themselves as his. They stood on his right side indicating their submissive nature. As such, they were easily captivated by him.[47] Śyāmalā vacillated between submissive and unsubmissive love, and Bhadrā, following the lead of Rādhā and standing in front of Kṛṣṇa, thought not "I am Kṛṣṇa's," but "Kṛṣṇa is mine." Although the love of Rādhā and her group of gopīs was unsubmissive, it delighted Kṛṣṇa much more.[48]

Rādhā and her friends Lalitā and Viśākhā stood at a distance from Kṛṣṇa. In loving anger, Rādhā bit her lip and stared at Kṛṣṇa, frowning her eyebrows, her glance cast like an arrow to wound him. Indeed, the power of that glance cast from the motionless Rādhā brought the pain of love to Kṛṣṇa, yet it left no visible wound. Not seeing Kṛṣṇa's submission to Rādhā, Lalitā stared at the lotus of Kṛṣṇa's face with unblinking eyes, as if in meditation. Yet her anger with Kṛṣṇa in aesthetic rapture far exceeded the joy of any yogī, to which her fixation is compared only for lack of a better metaphor.[49] Another of Rādhā's closest friends, Viśākhā, also fixed her eyes upon Kṛṣṇa. In doing so, she brought him within her heart, though physically she maintained a distance out of shyness. Her hairs stood erect as she experienced both union and separation.[50]

Seeing Kṛṣṇa before them once again, his beauty incomparable, all of the assembled gopīs joyfully experienced the great festival of his appearance. Their distress disappeared as the misery of people in general disappears upon achieving the association of an enlightened soul. Surrounded by the gopīs, Kṛṣṇa's beauty shone forth with even greater splendor, for these gopīs were none other than the potencies of the all-potent personified.

It is only by our potency that we are known. Our potency, or energy, is that by which we accomplish the deeds that we later become characterized by. To speak of a person is to speak of his energy. As such, the energetic source is known only by its energies. Although Kṛṣṇa is the supreme potent, the full extent of his standing will only be known by proper acquaintance with his potencies; in this case, the gopīs. They are constituted of his internal energy, and thus they reveal the inner heart of the Absolute. Standing in the gopīs' midst, the all-beautiful shines more beautifully, for the Absolute, although one, does not love alone.[51]

Then Kṛṣṇa took the gopīs to the banks of the Yamunā, who with her thousands of wave-like hands had arranged the sand on her banks such that it was suitable for Kṛṣṇa's intentions. The breeze carried the aroma of the Yamunā's lotus flowers and the forest's flowers as they burst into bloom, creating a symphony of intoxicated bees humming in the spotlight of the autumn moon. In turn, the Yamunā herself, daughter of the sun, danced in the night's delight, and Kṛṣṇa reveled with his gopīs on the sandy shore of her riverbed.

Responding to Kṛṣṇa's desire alone, the forest created a scene suitable for the *rāsa* dance. Indeed, this forest grows only for his pleasure, as all of his abode exists for his pleasure alone. Thus the flowers burst into bloom, although ordinarily they would not have at this time. The entire forest and the night itself moved out of involuntary ecstasy (eightfold *sāttvika-bhāva*) in response to Kṛṣṇa's mood of love for Rādhā and the other gopīs.

The trees, standing as if stunned (*stambha*), cried sweet honey tears (*aśru*); the flowers erupted (*romāñca*) into bloom, and the soft breeze, the life air of the forest, carried Kṛṣṇa's feeling of love for the gopīs to every vine and flowering tree. The bees hummed in intoxication, making a sound that, although unintelligible (*svara-bheda*), was nonetheless beautiful. The dark night turned white (*vaivarṇya*) in the moon's rays, which shined brightly revealing the trembling (*kampa*) of the Yamunā's black waters, a veritable river of the perspiration (*sveda*) of the forest creatures, moved by love's emotion for the dark youth of Vraja. All that had transpired thus far in preparation for the *rāsa* dance caused time to lose consciousness (*pralaya*), for the night should have ended long ago. Instead, in its unconsciousness, time stood still, facilitating the climax of this *līlā* of love.

Observing the surroundings and Kṛṣṇa's indications of love, the gopīs realized that they were about to experience the fulfillment of their desires. Their wildest dreams were about to come true. With their heartache vanquished, they realized the limit of sacred literature's advocacy. As the Vedas are eternal, every time Kṛṣṇa appears within the world they also manifest, and the deities presiding over them in each manifestation ultimately attain Kṛṣṇa's love, acquiring transcendental bodies as gopīs.[52] In this way, both theoretically and by practical example, the Vedas instruct human society about their conclusion: Love beyond knowledge is itself the highest knowledge.

As the gopīs and Kṛṣṇa gathered along the Yamunā, the younger *mañjarī* gopīs of Rādhā arranged a seat for Kṛṣṇa with their shawls. He whose partial manifestation sits in the hearts of the yogīs sat in the midst of these cowherd girls and appeared more splendid due to the ornament of their presence. Indeed, all of the beauty within the phenomenal world appeared to rest in him alone, for it is ultimately his *parā-śakti* that is responsible for the beauty of the world. This *parā-śakti* also rests in him in eternity, making him ever more beautiful.[53] Vṛndā devī, the forest gopī, orchestrated the forest deities in offering items to enhance the mood of love. They brought garlands, camphor, sandalwood paste mixed with various wonderful scents, and other items appropriate for love. Accepting these items graciously, Kṛṣṇa began to joke with the younger gopīs.

The *mañjarīs* of Rādhā, although very pleased with Kṛṣṇa's talks, indicated that before the *rāsa* dance could proceed, Kṛṣṇa needed to explain himself. With clever speech concealing their inner motive, Rādhā's *mañjarīs* asked Kṛṣṇa to answer a riddle concerning the nature of love. The gopīs asked about three types of lovers, yet Kṛṣṇa responded describing seven kinds of love. Then he described the nature of his love for them, revealing, in doing so, the glory of their own love.[54]

The *mañjarīs* said:

Some love only those who love them,
while others love even those who love them not.
Still others love neither those who love them,
nor those that do not.

In questioning Kṛṣṇa thus, the gopīs wanted to know what kind of lover he was. Why had he not reciprocated their love, leaving them to search desperately for him in the night, and why had he abandoned even Rādhā? In answer, Kṛṣṇa revealed that he left them only to shed light on the virtue of their love, for which no appropriate reciprocation is possible. That love is itself the highest gain.

Kṛṣṇa said:

Those who love others
only when others love, love very small
Dharma they know not, nor friendship do they call.

Without perceiving self-benefit in love,
they do not love at all.

Those merciful, like parents to their children,
love others even when they don't get love in return;
such lovers serve the truth of faultless religion.

Self-satisfied, ungrateful, materially fulfilled, the envious,
all these love neither those who love them,
nor those inimical.

Why do I not reciprocate
when others' love is true?
I want that love to grow
as one once rich, then poor
desires wealth more so.

You girls who for my sake alone
left world, the Vedas, and your own,
I left, only that your love for me would grow.
I never stopped loving you,
forgive me, now you know
just what your love has shown.

The debt incurred I cannot pay
in a life of Brahmā's time,

More than this, what can I say?
Your love for me itself is more
than I in mystic way.

The gopīs questioned Kṛṣṇa with a view to understand his love for them. They spoke of three types of lovers: those who love others only when they reciprocate, those who love others even when they do not reciprocate, and those who do not reciprocate in either case. Kṛṣṇa explained that those who love only when others reciprocate, in actuality do not love at all. Their love is selfish. Those who love even when they get nothing in return are merciful and love in accordance with *dharma*. Those who do not care for the love of others or for those who do not love them are of four types. The materially fulfilled, the ungrateful, the envious, and the self-realized, all for different reasons, do not reciprocate in love.

Hearing Kṛṣṇa's response, the gopīs thought that Kṛṣṇa did not fit any of these descriptions. They reasoned that while Kṛṣṇa is a knower of values and thus might love for the sake of reciprocation, he was at the same time righteous, or *dharmic*. Thus he was neither of these two. Nor could he be described as materially fulfilled or self-satisfied, for he had called them to him on this night. Since he did return, he was not ungrateful, nor was he envious of his superiors, for there is no one superior to him. Considering all of this, they were forced to conclude that Kṛṣṇa was in a class of his own, and this is what Kṛṣṇa had implied. What type of lover was he? He was a lover in the true sense of the term, a connoisseur of love, *rasa-rāja*. He loved only for the sake of love's increase, and because he witnessed their love to be beyond all comparison, he loved their love and desired that love himself.

Thus Kṛṣṇa revealed the glory of the gopīs' love, which he himself bowed to. Although it is the promise of Kṛṣṇa in *Gītopaniṣad* that he will reciprocate in love proportionate to his devotees loving surrender,[55] the gopīs had exhausted his capacity to reciprocate. Their love is thus beyond the reach of the Vedas themselves. Conquered by their love, Kṛṣṇa, the supreme Vedāntist, admitted that their love is more worshippable than even him. The attainment of such love is thus the zenith of transcendental culture. Witnessing the glory of this love while hiding, Kṛṣṇa himself desired to experience it. Herein, we find the acme of the love life of the Absolute: a union between energetic source and energy that produces further dynamic expression. This expression is Śrī Caitanya—the descent of Kṛṣṇa in the ecstasy of Rādhā. Śyāma, the color of love, became fair, the color of compassion, when Kṛṣṇa desired to experience Rādhā's love. This third person is Śrī Caitanya, the dynamic combination of Rādhā and Kṛṣṇa.[56] Through Śrī Caitanya's followers the secret of this love can be known by all.

Prema, the highest love, by nature hides itself. As love is a secret, a private affair, so too is the highest love kept hidden by the gopīs. If the selfless nature of the gopīs' love should be verbalized by them, that love would be diminished in stature.

Love's candle burns bright in lover's hearts
to set aglow those chamber's darkest parts;
if one should bring it out the verbal door,
pride's wind blows and it glows no more.[57]

Rather than verbalize the truth of their love, the gopīs do just the opposite, speaking and acting as though they are selfishly motivated. The union in love between Rādhā and Kṛṣṇa thus hides itself, manifesting overtly as something most selfish.

For a young married girl of Vedic culture to steal away into the night to rendezvous with a paramour is the height of selfishness. Driven by the selfishness of lust, a young girl is inconsiderate of her family's social reputation, her husband's feelings, and the injunctions of the sacred literature that call her to dignity and the truth of ultimate reality. Such appears to be the love of the gopīs for Kṛṣṇa. Yet their love is in truth the highest, most secret love camouflaging itself. While externally the gopīs appear self-centered, within they are motivated by *samartha-rati,*[58] or competent love, capable of fully satisfying Kṛṣṇa. The hidden mentality of the gopīs is, "We must increase Kṛṣṇa's pleasure in a new and special way," and in this they are most expert. Thus the *līlā* moves eternally, as the Absolute enjoys its own joy and in doing so hides itself from us, even when it makes its appearance in the world of our sense perception.

We can just imagine then the nature of the descent of Śrī Caitanya, who, in pursuing the glory of Rādhā's love, reveals it to the entire world. He did this principally through Śrī Rūpa Goswāmī. Although Kṛṣṇa proclaims the glory of Rādhā's and the gopīs' love in his *Bhāgavata* speech, Rūpa Goswāmī has amplified that glory under Śrī Caitanya's influence. It is the love role of Śrī Rūpa in his perfected gopī form as Rūpa Mañjarī that we are to follow if we are to taste the highest love of the soul.

RĀSA DANCE

After Kṛṣṇa revealed his heart to the gopīs, they felt reassured. Not only had their pangs of separation been mitigated in his presence, they were free now from the fear that he might again disappear. They knew that he was theirs, and they reached out and lovingly touched him.

Kṛṣṇa then began the *rāsa* dance, instructing the jewel-like gopīs to link their arms together, forming a necklace of pearls around the sapphire of himself. In order to share himself with all of the gopīs, Kṛṣṇa produced expansions of his own form, such that a Kṛṣṇa-sapphire became faceted between each gopī-pearl of this necklace of love, the *rāsa-maṇḍala*.

When Kṛṣṇa mystically expanded himself to appear between each gopī, each gopī thought that Kṛṣṇa was dancing with her alone. Kṛṣṇa's mystical expansions are examples of his ability to expand himself into innumerable forms, all nondifferent from himself (*prābhava-prakāśa*).[59]

While Kṛṣṇa expanded himself between every two gopīs, he simultaneously stood in the center of the *rāsa-maṇḍala* with only Rādhā, such that it appeared as though his dance with all of the gopīs was intended to ornament the jewel of his love for her. Although he danced with all of the gopīs simultaneously, his dancing with the others when compared to his dancing with Rādhā was like action (*kriyā-śakti*) in relation to consciousness (*jñāna-śakti*). Without consciousness, what is the value of action?

As the *rāsa* dance commenced, the gopīs' ankle bells, bangles, and bracelets shimmered, keeping time with their steps and orchestrating a concert that even the heavenly denizens had never witnessed. All of nature's movements personified—the gods of sun, moon, wind, and stars, along with their wives, the goddesses—became captivated by the dancing of the gopīs and Gopāla.

The gods and goddesses turned earthward, where love finds its fullest expression. The dance of Kṛṣṇa and the gopīs thus demonstrated that it is indeed love that makes the world go round. All stopped at the sight and sound of this wonderful dance of aesthetic rapture, although its Vedānta, its truth, was not easily understood. Yet the gods and goddesses gave testimony to its sanctity, as heaven looked down to look up beyond itself.

Celestial airplanes lined the sky, forming a concert auditorium in which patrons played their own instruments in musical accompaniment. Thus the eternal dance of love gave birth to *rāga* and *rāginī* in all of their 16,000 principal expressions,[60] and all forms of classical dance stepped into the world as well. *Rāsa-līlā* aside, every movement of the gopīs was itself dance and every word song.[61] Thus the mind returns unsuccessful in trying to imagine the nature of their *actual* song and dance, and words fail to describe them.[62] Flowers rained from the sky as the heavenly denizens announced the religious nature of the affair, even without fully understanding its import.

The gopīs sang in praise of Kṛṣṇa, and as they danced they expressed their thoughts with their hands, eyebrows, and smiles. Their tightly tied belts and braids loosened in their mirth. Their breasts and earrings swung to and fro. Thus innumerable fair gopīs appeared like lightning bolts amidst a mass of dark Kṛṣṇa-clouds, misty with their own perspiration, thundering with the sounds of their voices.

Then Viśākhā sang in accompaniment with Kṛṣṇa. Her song was a pure and unmixed rendering (*svara-jāti*) of the scale. This amazed Kṛṣṇa, for who but he, from whom these notes originate, could sing them so purely? Thinking, "Other than me, no one knows the real nature of music; therefore, how is she singing so perfectly?" Kṛṣṇa thus remarked, "Excellent, well done!" Then Lalitā echoed Viśākhā singing a steady rhythm (*dhruva-tāla*), and Kṛṣṇa appreciated this as much if not more.

Rādhā was pleased at Kṛṣṇa's reaction to the singing of her friends, thus Kṛṣṇa relished their song even more, indicating so through his flute. Rādhā, growing tired from the dancing, threw her arm around Kṛṣṇa's shoulder, as her bracelets loosened and flowers fell from her hair. Although Kṛṣṇa is known to exhibit four arms in places other than Vraja, at this time Kṛṣṇa played his flute and simultaneously embraced all the gopīs with only two arms. Such is the opulence of love that far exceeds all other opulences.

Śyāmala's hair stood on end as Kṛṣṇa rested his arm smeared with sandalwood on her shoulder while holding a lotus in his hand. In joy, she kissed his hand.[63] Śaibyā, whose cheeks lit up with the reflection of her earrings as they tossed about in dancing, rested her cheek on Kṛṣṇa. Then Kṛṣṇa gave from his mouth the betel he had chewed, placing it into hers. Candrāvalī, becoming fatigued as she danced and sang with her ankle and waist bells jingling, placed Kṛṣṇa's hand on her breast. Thus the gopīs, having attained as their lover he whose love is ever sought after by the goddess of fortune, sang his glories with their arms wrapped around his neck in intimate embrace.

The beauty of the gopīs' faces was enhanced by the lotus flowers behind their ears, the locks of hair decorating their faces, and the drops of perspiration on their cheeks. The music of their various ornaments was accompanied by the humming of swarms of bees. Thus the husband of the goddess of fortune played in the company of these young girls of Vraja, embracing them, caressing them, and glancing at them with his broad playful smiles as if he were a child playing with his own reflection.[64]

The gopīs are described here as reflections of Brahman, through whom he enjoys himself in eternity. Through the gopīs, Kṛṣṇa sees and experiences himself more fully. Although they are different from him, they are simultaneously nondifferent from him (*acintya-bhedābheda*), being his *śaktis*. Just as a person looking in a mirror sees himself as he could otherwise not, Kṛṣṇa looking at the gopīs sees himself through his *śakti* without the manifestation of which he could not experience himself so completely.

In the joy of their association with Kṛṣṇa's body, the gopīs could not prevent their braids and garments from loosening. Their garlands and ornaments scattered in their delight. As the devas' wives looked on from their aerial seats, they swooned and became passionately aroused. The moon and his entourage of stars, astonished, paused in their flight for a night of Brahmā.[65]

It is the moon alone who has first claim to virgin girls.[66] Along with him, his wives, the stars, who unlike him are spotless in character, were amazed to see the spotless moon, Kṛṣṇacandra, dancing so with the star-like gopīs. It was as if the supreme heaven had appeared on earth, causing the ordinary heavenly constellation to look in awe. One wonders if the moon and stars' perpetual movement is but a reaction to the ultimate heaven they experienced on earth that autumn night. It is common knowledge that the gopīs are named after the constellations, yet uncommon knowledge suggests just the opposite.

Gradually the gopīs' dance of love fatigued them. It was not, however, the dance itself that caused this as much as their further interest in love, for the body moves in accordance with the mind. Their minds racing for love, Kṛṣṇa suggested a game of hide and seek in which he hid and all the gopīs individually found him. He who is satisfied in himself alone thus met privately with each gopī. Realizing their fatigue and more their interest in love, Kṛṣṇa removed the perspiration from their brows with his loving hand. He adjusted the gopīs' garments, addressing their state of disarray as well as their desire. As for their tears, he replaced them with his own. And the gopīs, noticing his fatigue, reciprocated with him.

Like a lordly elephant, Kṛṣṇa then entered the Yamunā with the gopīs, who followed him as she elephants follow the best of the herd. Kṛṣṇa's garland had been crushed by the dance and colored by the vermilion on the gopīs' breasts. Its scent thus enhanced, it attracted a swarm of bees, who sang like Gandharvas. Thus Kṛṣṇa and the gopīs relaxed within the waters of the Yamunā and then sported further, all in apparent violation of moral and Vedic injunctions. The gopīs splashed Kṛṣṇa from all sides, gazing at him with love, as the *devas* worshipped him, showering flowers from the heavens.

The gopīs massaged Kṛṣṇa, and the elephant-like Lord left the Yamunā and attired himself in his best dress. Together with the gopīs and accompanied further by the singing bees, Kṛṣṇa sported throughout the forest, the night air filled with the scent of all the forest flowers and lilies. As the night came to a close, Kṛṣṇa advised the gopīs to return home, in order to keep their affair a secret and thus preserve its thrilling sweetness. They returned with great reluctance, compelled by fear of their elders. That fear only appeared to defeat their passion for his company. Indeed, it actually intensified their passion, for as they moved from union to separation, their hearts grew fonder. Thus although free from all material desire, Kṛṣṇa enjoyed the moonlit autumn night that so inspires poetic description of truth and beauty (*rasāśraya*).

CHAPTER THREE

The Sacred Path

O rite and ritual
light to reality,
what is your heart?
The river runs freely,
I bathe with regularity;
the bell rings, all rise,
for whom doth thou toll?

Then rhyme and rhythm,
the drum beats, and
we are driven to dance
and sing in abandon.
What merry have you made,
and why do I ask on?

O rite and ritual
your performance habitual,
when will we part
the door between reality
and see your heart of spontaneity?

ONCE A YOUNG LADY stole into the night to meet her lover while her husband was away from home. Running in the dark, blinded by her love, she accidentally tripped over a sage engaged in meditation. Disturbed, the sage condemned the lady for both her rendezvous and her recklessness.

After meeting her lover, the lady returned home along the same path, more awake now to her surroundings, having put her love to rest for the time being. Upon reaching the sage, she greeted him with the traditional "*namaskāra*."

Astounded at her audacity, the sage condemned her for having broken his meditation while treading the path of irreligion. Characteristically denying that which she was involved in, she pressed the sage as to when it was that she broke his meditation. When the sage related the details, she honestly admitted to remembering nothing of the sort. Astounded, the sage learned something about meditation that night.

This story is not intended to sing the virtues of immorality. It does, however, instruct us on the intensity of passionate paramour love. The paramour lover was so absorbed in her rendezvous that she lost all external consciousness. The sage involved in traditional meditation, on the other hand, was easily disturbed from his practice. Thus the potential for absorbing one's consciousness through passionate love is immense. If then one could make the Absolute the object of passionate love, this would arguably be the highest form of meditation. Such is possible when the Absolute is conceived as Kṛṣṇa, the emporium of *rasa*. Yet to love him passionately, one must learn to live in the world of consciousness, not the world of matter. One must realize the Brahman in oneself, one's soul, to love the Param Brahman, Śrī Kṛṣṇa. Rūpa Goswāmī called the means to do so *rāgānuga-sādhana-bhakti*.

Before discussing the practice of *rāgānuga-bhakti*, it is prudent to discuss the scriptural basis for such practice. *Rāgānuga-bhakti* is an advocacy of lawless spiritual love, and its validity has been questioned by a number of morally stout religious men and women, both in India and abroad. In India, reference to sacred literature is common. If one cannot support one's view with reference to such texts, one's argument does not carry much weight.

Sacred literature forms a vital part of religious life in India. The guru and other saints are considered to be like the two eyes of the *sādhaka* (practitioner), who is asleep to his spiritual prospect. Without such eyes, one cannot see. Yet without the sun, eyes are useless. Scripture has thus been compared to the sun, by whose light the truth is made known.

Sacred literature speaks to us on a number of levels. By evaluating the psyche of individuals and thus their karmic propensity for action, it provides codes of working direction. Through such codes, it dictates a social structure. However, regardless of each person's role in society, sacred literature puts forward a common goal of life for all. This goal is liberation from material existence, and ultimately attainment of love of God.

In the course of encouraging the general populace in the direction of love of God, the texts are so arranged as to offer short-term goals along the way that are easier to attain and of more immediate importance to those absorbed in material consciousness. For example, the general public is encouraged through the majority of the texts to pursue heavenly pleasures in the next life. Heaven, however, is a higher material realm, and although it is a pious attainment, it is not a permanent resting place for the soul. Gradually one realizes this and listens more carefully to the texts, at which point one finds that beyond heaven lies liberation. This liberation is of five kinds. Four of them are forms of God-realization,[1] while one amounts to liberation from material existence without realization of the form and qualities of Godhead.

The means to reach heaven is the path of karma, or good works. Knowledge and its corollary, renunciation, when mixed with devotion, lead to one of the five types of liberation. The greater the balance of devotion in the recipe of renunciation and devotion, the closer one comes to God. When one uses devotion only as a means to liberation with little interest in devotion itself, this leads to realization of the formless aspect of God. When devotion is considered the means to eternally associate with God, this leads to one of the other four types of God-conscious liberation. All these paths require adherence to the sacred texts. The religious are bound by laws governing this world. The renunciates seeking liberation and devotees interested in the same are bound either by the texts governing knowledge and renunciation of work or by the texts governing devotion. Where, then, in all of this is there room for a path that is not regulated by the sacred texts—lawless passionate love transcending even ritualistic devotion (*vaidhi-bhakti*)? Is there scriptural support for *rāgānuga-bhakti*?

Śrī Jīva Goswāmī has established in *Bhakti-sandarbha* that *rāgānuga-bhakti* is the purport of the *Bhāgavatam*. Yet the *Bhāgavatam*'s claims as to our potential for intimacy with God are such that they have caused people to question the validity of even the *Bhāgavatam* itself.

When the British came to India to give the "good news" of the "one true religion," they first attempted to understand the sacred texts of the Hindus. When the Orientalists, the first Indologists, attempted to do the same, they did so with a strong Christian bias. When they came across Vaiṣṇavism in their studies, they remarked that it was the closest religion to Christianity. They acknowledged many parallels between this monotheistic religion of grace and their own gospel. Yet close was not enough. Furthermore, when they came upon the *Bhāgavatam* and its *rāsa-līlā*, they condemned the Vaiṣṇavas to hell along with everyone else.

In Kṛṣṇa *līlā* they felt they found the strongest justification for condemnation of Indian religious life. So strong was their condemnation that Hindus themselves were hard-pressed to defend their apparently misbehaved Rādhā and Kṛṣṇa.

In time, pious Hindus fought back, defending their rich spiritual heritage. Hindu reformers at the turn of the twentieth century formed movements like the Ārya Samāja and Brahmo Samāja. Appreciating Christianity, they canvassed for a Hinduism that was as Christian as possible. Their ideal was Kṛṣṇa the statesman and spiritual teacher of the *Mahābhārata* and *Gītā*. They scorned Rādhā-Kṛṣṇa and the *Bhāgavatam*, considering them interpolations not of divine origin. Even the renowned pioneer of *rāgānuga-bhakti* in the West, Bhaktivinoda Ṭhākura, admits in his early writing to have been raised with a negative bias toward the *Bhāgavatam*.

It was only when Bhaktivinoda Ṭhākura acquired a copy of the *Caitanya-caritāmṛta*, the 17th-century hagiography of Śrī Caitanya, that he came to see the *Bhāgavatam* in its true light. Therein he learned of the life and precepts of Śrī Caitanya. In outward appearance, Śrī Caitanya was a strict renunciate, his moral character beyond reproach. Yet inwardly Śrī Caitanya's mind was absorbed in meditation upon the love *līlās* of Rādhā-Kṛṣṇa. Bhaktivinoda realized the impossibility of mental preoccupation with the amorous affairs of a young boy and girl and complete sexual abstinence. He realized through Śrī Caitanya's example that the *līlās* of Rādhā-Kṛṣṇa were supramundane, and in *Caitanya-caritāmṛta* he found a wealth of philosophy to support this notion as well as the Gauḍīya conviction that Śrī Caitanya's own *līlā* mystically paralleled that of Rādhā-Kṛṣṇa. Thus his eyes were opened to aesthetic Vedānta, and he dove deeply into the lake of Śrī Caitanya's precepts and pastimes. Although Kṛṣṇa *līlā* historically appears before the appearance of Śrī Caitanya, it is Śrī Caitanya who is the giver of that *līlā* to the world. First we must have the giver and only then the gift.

O swan of my mind!
Swim, swim in the nectar lake
of immortal Caitanya līlā.
From there, in hundreds of streams,

and all ten directions,
flows the essence of bliss
that is Rādhā-Kṛṣṇa līlā.[2]

Bhaktivinoda Ṭhākura proceeded to write about, practice, and broadcast the divine message of *rāgānuga-bhakti*. It is to him and his followers that the world is most indebted for having received the good news of passionate love of Kṛṣṇa. With the British empire, upon which at one time the sun never set, now shrunken to a cold island in the Atlantic, Christ forsaken for Kṛṣṇa by many more in the West than Vaiṣṇavas converted to Christianity, and Indologists now extolling the virtues of the *Bhāgavatam*, the victory of *rāgānuga-bhakti* is a sweet one. Such was predicted by Śrī Caitanya himself, a prediction that although beginning to manifest, is still in the process of unfolding.[3]

Śrī Caitanya embodied *rāgānuga-bhakti* in its perfection. His immediate followers, the Goswāmīs, under his direction articulated the path of *rāgānuga-bhakti*, demonstrating its scriptural basis. They revealed that the path of lawless passionate love of God was not only based on the sacred texts, but was their essential and highest advocacy. Passionate love is a life above law, where love need not be regulated, its current so strong.

Among the literature of the Goswāmīs, there are several works that articulate the path of passionate love. The path of *rāgānuga* is discussed in 25 verses of Rūpa Goswāmī's *Bhakti-rasāmṛta-sindhu*. Jīva Goswāmī concludes his *Bhakti-sandarbha* with a description of *rāgānuga-bhakti*, and Viśvanātha Cakravartī delineates the path in his *Rāga-vartma-candrikā*. These are the three most well-known texts describing the practice of *rāgānuga-bhakti*, all of which are supported with evidence from *Śrīmad-Bhāgavatam*, as well as a wide range of sacred literature. Once one's eyes have been opened by the light of the Goswāmīs' vision, it is hard to imagine how one could not have seen that which, once illumined, seems to spring from every passionate page of *Śrīmad-Bhāgavatam*. Jīva Goswāmī's *Bhakti-sandarbha* in particular makes evident the *Bhāgavatam*'s sole advocacy of passionate love for Kṛṣṇa.

Vedānta is not restricted to the study of the *śruti*, or Upaniṣads, alone. The corollaries of the Upaniṣads, such as the Purāṇas, are also valid evidence (*pramāṇa*).

Drawing upon the entirety of sacred literature provides considerable evidence for the advocacy of passionate love of God. However, it will suffice herein to draw from the sacred texts that are most well known and readily available. *Vedānta-sūtra* (3.3.19) explains that *rāgānuga-bhakti* is appropriate because it is mentioned in the scripture that meditation upon the Absolute as master, friend, son, lover, and so on brings about liberation. Here the *sūtra* informs us that just as it is appropriate to meditate upon the Absolute as perfection and bliss, it is appropriate to meditate on God as the soul's lover.

Support from the *śruti* for this statement is found in the *Bhagavad-gītā*. In the 11th chapter of the *Gītā*, Kṛṣṇa revealed his cosmic form. While viewing that form, Arjuna tells Kṛṣṇa, "You alone are my father, mother, lover, friend, brother, and son." *Śrīmad-Bhāgavatam*, the essence of the *śruti* and Vyāsa's natural commentary on the *sūtras*, is more explicit, declaring that devotees become very dear to Kṛṣṇa by accepting him as teacher, friend, son, and lover. (SB. 3.25.38) The *Bhāgavatam*'s verse (11.12.8) commenting on the *sūtra* cited above says that the gopīs and all other inhabitants of Vṛndāvana, Kṛṣṇa's idyllic abode, attained perfection simply by thinking of him (as lover, etc.).

We can look further to the *Gītā* commentaries of the followers of Śrī Caitanya for a Upaniṣadic reading in support of *rāgānuga-bhakti*. The *Bhagavad-gītā* is widely accepted and often referred to as *Gītopaniṣad* to stress its importance and connection with Vedānta. Many of the verses in the *Gītā* bear resemblance to the statements of the Upaniṣads. The *Gītā* is considered by the Gauḍīyas to contain in seed that which manifests as the tree, flower, and fruit of actual spiritual life (*bhakti-rasa*) in the *Bhāgavatam*.

The *Gītopaniṣad* consists of 18 chapters. The first 6 deal with action (karma) in accordance with scripturally prescribed socio-religious roles. These 6 chapters teach one to perform prescribed actions in accordance with one's acquired nature, or karmic propensity, yet to renounce the fruit of one's actions. Beginning with the seventh chapter, Kṛṣṇa speaks directly about *bhakti*. In chapters 7 and 8 he speaks about *bhakti* mixed with karma, and *bhakti* mixed with *jñāna* (knowledge), respectively. In the ninth chapter, Kṛṣṇa speaks about pure devotion, free of desire born of karmic propensities and the desire for liberation. The chapter culminates in Kṛṣṇa's telling Arjuna to "always think of me. Become my devotee." He says that this is the most confidential knowledge. Finishing the chapter, enthused from speaking about such devotion, Kṛṣṇa continues to speak about the same in the tenth chapter. Verses 8 through 11 of the tenth chapter have been called the *catuḥ-śloki*, or 4 essential verses of the *Gītā*. Within these verses is a very deep secret. Kṛṣṇa speaks about both *sambandhānuga* and *kāmānuga*, Rūpa Goswāmī's two divisions of *rāgānuga-bhakti*.

In the first verse of the *Gītā*'s *catuḥ-sloki*, Kṛṣṇa describes himself as the source of everything. He who is the source of even the other *avatāras* is Kṛṣṇa, and we know about the kind of worship his intimate devotees perform. In this verse he mentions this intimate worship when he says *budhā-bhāva-samanvitāḥ*, one should worship with *bhāva*, also known as *rati*. This worship with great feeling for Kṛṣṇa is not awe and reverence, but *rāga-samanvitāḥ, rāgānuga-bhakti*. In the second of the four essential verses, Kṛṣṇa refers to his devotees with the words "*tuṣyanti*" and "*ramanti*." *Tuṣyanti* means nourishment, a reference to *bhakti-rasa* in servitude, friendship, and parental love in particular (*sambandha*). The general meaning of *ramanti* is "to take pleasure." However, it is at the same time a reference to the special type of pleasure a woman enjoys when she serves her lover. Thus in this verse Kṛṣṇa identifies those devotees who worship him with *bhāva*. They are the gopīs whose *bhāva* is *kṛṣṇa-rati* of conjugal love (*kāmānuga*).

In the next verse Kṛṣṇa says that those who are perpetually engaged in serving him with *prīti* (love) are guided by him (*buddhi-yoga*) from within their hearts so that they can come to him (*upayānti*). In closely analyzing this verse, a question arises. What is the need for knowledge of and guidance about how to come to Kṛṣṇa for those who perpetually love him? Thus what Kṛṣṇa is really telling Arjuna is that to those devotees just described as *ramanti*, who want to be his wives, he gives special knowledge (*buddhi-yoga*) to come to him as paramours. The word *upayānti* (come near) in this verse has been tied to *upapati*, "paramour."[4] Although pure souls can become wives of Kṛṣṇa in Dvārakā, where he is worshipped in knowledge of his ultimacy, the culture of such love is not *rāgānuga-bhakti*. Neither do such loving devotees need special knowledge (*buddhi-yoga*) to come to Kṛṣṇa (*upayānti*). This special knowledge is reserved for the gopīs, who even while realizing Kṛṣṇa *līlā* and participating in it, require secret knowledge to meet with him due to their apparent marriage to other men. If this verse does not refer to the Vraja-gopīs, to what then is the special knowledge (*buddhi-yoga*) referring? Why would devotees who love Kṛṣṇa constantly (*satata-yuktānām*), not merely purely but with *prīti* (the highest love), further require special knowledge (*buddhi-yoga*)? Such is the nature of *parakīya*, the paramour love of the gopīs for Kṛṣṇa in Vraja, in which secret rendezvous are required.

In the last of the four essential *Gītopaniṣad* verses, Kṛṣṇa continues to speak about the path of passionate love. Rendering it consistent with the spirit of *rāgānuga*, Kṛṣṇa says, "Conquered by the love of these devotees, I want their favor (*teṣām evānukampārtham*). Thus when they experience the dark night of the soul (*ajñāna-jaṁ tamaḥ*) born of my separation, I illuminate them by coming before them."[5] The *rāsa-pañcādhyāya* of the *Śrīmad-Bhāgavatam* provides many examples of this separation and reunion.

Later in the 12th chapter of the *Gītā*, Kṛṣṇa advocates devotion over the cultivation of abstract knowledge of the Absolute. He does this throughout the text, but in the 12th chapter, Arjuna asks Kṛṣṇa directly, "Which is better, devotion unto you or meditation on the unmanifest Absolute?" Kṛṣṇa answers in favor of devotion. He then goes on to speak of a gradation. First he says it is best to "just love me" (by fixing your mind on me, *mayy eva mana ādhatsva*). If one cannot do that, he says, "practice loving me" (*abhyāsa-yogena*). If this too is difficult, then "do my work" (*mat-karma-paramaḥ*). If this is not possible, then "do your own work, but offer the fruits of your work to me" (*sarva-karma-phala-tyāgam*).

Here Kṛṣṇa tells us that there are those who just love him. From the *Bhāgavatam*, wherein the life of Kṛṣṇa is described, we come to know who these people are. They are the gopīs and others who are always associated with him in Vraja, his eternal abode, which manifests on earth from time to time. Kṛṣṇa's associates are eternally linked with him in love.

We cannot just do as they do, for we are not yet qualified. Yet their example is best; therefore, it should be our ideal. This is the practice that Kṛṣṇa speaks of next, *abhyāsa-yogena*. In essence, he says, "Practice *rāgānuga-bhakti* by following those who love me." As we shall see, to do so exclusively also requires considerable qualification. Thus if one is not yet qualified to do so, Kṛṣṇa suggests that which, if done with a view to attain such love, will be most helpful. He says, "Do my work." This is an advocacy of the life of devotion regulated by scriptural injunctions, the life of ritualistic *bhakti*. If this too is not possible, Kṛṣṇa advises us to do our own work as ordained in the sacred literature in consideration of our karmic propensity, and in doing so, begin to offer the fruits of our efforts to him. As one does this, one gradually becomes free of the false sense of proprietorship that constitutes material life. One then moves to a life of devotion and gradually enters into the practice of *rāgānuga-bhakti* proper, by which one attains love of Kṛṣṇa. In all of this, Kṛṣṇa is saying, "The goal is to love me like my friends and gopīs of Vraja do."

In concluding his speech to Arjuna at the end of the *Gītā*, Kṛṣṇa again speaks directly about *rāgānuga-bhakti*. He reiterates his most confidential instruction given in the ninth chapter, "Always think of me." The example of this condition in which one's mind is given over to Kṛṣṇa is found in the *Bhāgavatam* in the lives of the gopīs. In the *Bhāgavatam*'s tenth canto, 46th chapter, Kṛṣṇa sends his friend Uddhava to Vraja from Dvārakā to bring a message to the gopīs, who have been living in separation from him for so long. At that time, Uddhava experienced the full purport of "always think of me" in the lives of the gopīs. He was so astounded to witness the nature of their absorption in Kṛṣṇa that he himself aspired to take birth in Vraja as a blade of grass just to be touched by their feet.[6] One must remember that Uddhava was already a great liberated devotee of Kṛṣṇa, confidential enough for Kṛṣṇa to have chosen him to deliver his message to the gopīs.

After telling Arjuna in a straightforward manner that the most confidential knowledge he had taught him thus far was "always think of me," Kṛṣṇa goes on to say something more. In his final instruction, he says, "Give up all varieties of *dharma* (religion) and just surrender; come to me. Don't worry about any sinful reactions incurred from ignoring all the sacred literature's religious injunctions, I will protect you." In effect, Kṛṣṇa is saying, "If you always think of me (which is only possible by love), you need not bother with all other rules and regulations, for they are meant to promote this love of myself above all other things."

In making this extraordinary claim, the *Gītā* comes to a close. Kṛṣṇa becomes silent; his instructions are complete. His silence here, however, is a result of the inner significance of his own statement. When Kṛṣṇa said, "Come to me," he used the verb *vraja*. Yet Vraja, as we know, when used as a noun refers to Kṛṣṇa's land of love. The verb *vraja,* although grammatically referring to something else, nonetheless brought Vraja to Kṛṣṇa's mind. This is an instance of *alaṅkāra,* or Sanskrit rhetoric. Here *dhvani,* the ornamental suggestion by which the sound of a word echoes its sense, is employed. Because the sound of the word *vraja* can bring to mind its primary meaning (for Kṛṣṇa) as a reference to Vraja, the hidden meaning here is "come to me in Vraja."[7] This is possible only through *rāgānuga-bhakti*, in which scriptural guidelines are ultimately transcended and devotees like the gopīs may appear even to transgress them. When Kṛṣṇa said *vraja*, his mind went to the gopīs, and thus he could not speak any further. This understanding of the Vedānta of *Gītopaniṣad* is certainly full of aesthetic charm, both beautiful and bewildering. If one wants to find out more about this beautiful truth and the Vraja where Kṛṣṇa himself loses his mind, one must go to *Śrīmad-Bhāgavatam*.

In the *Bhāgavatam* chapters dealing with the *rāsa-līlā*, a question is raised by King Parīkṣit.[8] Parīkṣit heard the *Bhāgavatam* from the renounced Śukadeva. The king asked questions, and the sage answered them. In this section, Parīkṣit pointedly asks Śukadeva, "How is it that the gopīs, unaware as they were of Kṛṣṇa's supreme position, could have attained love of God while approaching him with what appears to be lust?" At this question Śukadeva became irritated with his student. He refers him back to the seventh canto of the text, wherein he says that he already explained this point.

In the beginning of the seventh canto, sage Nārada is speaking with King Yudhiṣṭhira. There he extols the virtues of those inimical to Kṛṣṇa, for they become so obsessed with thoughts of him. If only, Nārada laments, he could be so mentally absorbed in thinking of Kṛṣṇa. Nārada goes on to say that those whose minds become fully absorbed in Kṛṣṇa—either through passion, envy, fear, affection, or devotion—attain him. The emphasis here is on total mental absorption. Then he offers examples of people who became mentally absorbed in Kṛṣṇa through passion, envy, fear, affection, and devotion. With regard to passion, he cites the gopīs. The import of these verses is that if through intense envy, fear, affection, or ritualistic devotion directed toward Kṛṣṇa one can attain him, how much more can one attain Kṛṣṇa when one's mind is absorbed in Kṛṣṇa through passionate love. This "much more" amounts to entrance into Kṛṣṇa's Vraja *līlā*. Those who absorb themselves in any other way still attain Kṛṣṇa, but do so to a lesser extent. In pointing this out, the *Bhāgavatam* advocates *rāgānuga-bhakti*. Śukadeva thus answers the king with a reference to what he had instructed earlier, and then goes on to further establish the glory of the gopīs' love with a verse that parallels his verse in the seventh canto.[9]

In the final chapter of the *rāsa-pañcādhyāya*, King Parīkṣit again questions Śukadeva along the same lines. He asks how Kṛṣṇa, who is the very bridge of *dharma*, *dharma-setu*, could be engaged in apparent adultery. Śukadeva answers him and then concludes the *rāsa-pañcādhyāya* with an extraordinary statement. Śukadeva says, "Anyone who faithfully hears or describes the Lord's playful affairs with the young gopīs of Vṛndāvana will attain the Lord's pure devotional service. Thus he will quickly become sober and conquer lust, the disease of the heart."[10] The implication of this verse is that even the vilest person, if he hears with faith from the proper person about the *līlās* of Rādhā-Kṛṣṇa, will attain *bhakti,* and his lust will be vanquished. *Rāga* for Kṛṣṇa will cure the *roga* (disease) of the heart.

We must remember that sacred literature is such because it is backed by God. This is the reason why one advances in religious life by following scriptural injunctions. *Rāgānuga-bhakti* does not advocate breaking or forgoing the scriptural injunctions; it advocates directly pleasing the person from whom their power is derived. *Rāgānuga-bhakti* is not a disregard for scripture, for it is indeed only from the scripture that we come to know of such a path, *śāstra-yonitvāt.*[11] It is, however, a path upon which the *dharma-śāstra* has no bearing. *Bhakti-śāstra,* which governs *vaidhi-bhakti,* on the other hand, must be followed by those desiring to attain *rāga* for Kṛṣṇa. Although *rāgānuga* is superior to *vaidhi-bhakti,* it does not disregard the injunctions of *vaidhi-bhakti*. *Rāgānuga-sādhakas* are advised to follow the injunctions of *vaidhi-bhakti* with a different motive than those on the path of *vaidhi-bhakti*. Perfect adherence to the injunctions is the goal of *vaidhi-bhakti*, while following in the footsteps of Kṛṣṇa's eternal associates in Vṛndāvana is the goal of *rāgānuga-sādhakas*. In order to follow them properly, one should adopt the regulations of *vaidhi-bhakti* to the extent of, and with the same ideal as, the compilers of the *rāgānuga-bhakti-śāstras*. The immortal Six Goswāmīs of Vṛndāvana, after carefully studying all of the sacred literary heritage of India, wrote extensively to make clear the path of *rāgānuga-bhakti*. In so doing, they demonstrated that passionate love for Kṛṣṇa is the very heart of sacred literature.

The Sanskrit word *rāga* means attachment. It is derived from the verbal root *rañj*, "to color." Thus one who has *rāga* is colored by attachment. The soul's attachment to non-eternal objects propels its material sojourn. This attachment is deeply rooted in lifetimes of material association. Our associations and experiences in material life form impressions on our soul called *saṁskāras*. Because of these *saṁskāras*, people appear naturally inclined toward one or another type of lifestyle. They appear spontaneously attracted to various sense objects. This spontaneity, a product of material association, is problematic, for even if one becomes inclined to divine life through spiritual association, one spontaneously moves in the opposite direction. The minds of such people move like an unattended steering wheel. *Rāga* in the wrong direction is our disease. This is so much so that many have argued well for the eradication of all *rāga* in the pursuit of reality. Yet it is *rāga* that gives rise to the spontaneous action that we sense is at the heart of ultimate reality. If life is about love, *rāga* must be more than a rogue in the eternal drama. *Rāga* has its purified expression in transcendence, wherein the object of passionate attachment is Kṛṣṇa.

Rāgānuga-sādhana-bhakti, the path of passionate love, constitutes awakening *rāga* for Kṛṣṇa and cultivating it by following (*anuga*) in the wake of those who swim and dive deeply in the ocean of *bhakti-rasa*. Such people are called *rāgātmikas*, or those in whom *rāga* is inborn. *Rāga* for Kṛṣṇa is their very *ātmā*, or soul. They are not *sādhakas*, or practitioners; they experience *sādhya*, love's perfection. Kṛṣṇa's eternal associates, and the gopīs in particular, are examples of *rāgātmikas*. They embody the eternal ideal of the practitioners, who through hearing and chanting about the gopīs, purify their consciousness and imbibe the gopīs' spiritual emotions.[12] Thus the ideal of the practitioner is not a product of his or her practice. It is an eternally existing emotional reality; however, there are practices one can engage in that help qualify one for experiencing it. Such practices are taught by the spiritual preceptor, who represents the ideal embodied in the gopīs. Thus hearing from the guru who awakens initial faith and taking initiation and instruction from him constitute the beginning of the path of passionate love.

The Western religious romance with the East over the last 30 years or more has fallen short of a wedding for a number of reasons. Not the least among them is the fact that vows to the guru go against the grain of Western culture. Gurus breaking their own vows has not helped the affair. Yet the principle of accepting a realized guide is not to be dispensed with just because some of those who pose themselves as such fall short. Nor does insistence upon a Westernized version of spiritual life that dispenses with the necessity of accepting a guru go very far, for spiritual life is about change, radical change. We are to change radically, while the tradition, in adapting itself culturally, does so minimally. Details can be changed, but not principles. This may be strong language for some, yet the very notion of guru as understood in the path of passionate love may soften the blow to our ego.

The language used by Rūpa Goswāmī in describing service to the guru is itself endearing. Śrī Rūpa says we should serve the guru in affectionate intimacy.[13] In *rāgānuga-bhakti*, the guru is a master of service and love. Thus only the mature servant can act as guru and embody loving service. One who serves as guru is not God, but a lover of God, and the dearmost friend of the disciple. Under such a guru's guidance, love of Kṛṣṇa descends within the disciple's heart. This love, not being a product of spiritual practice, can never be evolved from within, for the relationship must be initiated by Kṛṣṇa. It is the prerogative of the Absolute, and not our right. Fortunately, Kṛṣṇa is the personification of affection and love. As such, he is more than willing to initiate a relationship with us, and thus he commissions his agents for this purpose.

Under the guidance of the guru, the disciple learns the preliminary practices, which include a hygienic regime and code of moral conduct conducive to the inner practice of meditation. From the guru, the disciple receives a rosary of 108 beads fashioned from the wood of the sacred basil tree (*tulasī*). The disciple adorns his neck with smaller *tulasī* beads and marks his body with *tilaka*, a mark made with a type of clay gathered from the sacred place of Kṛṣṇa's earthly birth. This *tilaka* mark distinguishes one lineage from another and outwardly designates the body as a temple of God. On his rosary, the disciple performs *japa*, an inaudible utterance of the names of Kṛṣṇa. He also learns to chant the sacred names of Kṛṣṇa congregationally. After a degree of inner purity is attained, the guru imparts the *kāma gayatrī mantra* into the right ear of the disciple, along with other esoteric mantras consisting primarily of Kṛṣṇa's names.

More than anything else, practitioners of passionate love chant Kṛṣṇa's name within the mantric formula of what has been called the *tāraka-brahma-mahā-mantra*. *Tāraka* comes from the verbal root *tṛ*, to cross over. The great (*mahā*) mantra is found in the *Kali-santaraṇa*

Upaniṣad.[14] It is mentioned therein in the context of Brahmā answering a query of sage Nārada. Nārada asked Brahmā the means of deliverance in the Kali-yuga, the present age of hypocrisy. Brahmā replied that the principal means of deliverance is chanting the names of God. Nārada then inquired, "Which names of God?" for indeed he has many. Brahmā then uttered the *mahā-mantra* and spoke of its efficacy. He told Nārada that the arrangement of the three names—Hare, Rāma, and Kṛṣṇa—grouped in this mantra into eight couplets, destroy all of the negative influences of Kali-yuga when chanted. He said that this was the verdict of all the sacred literature.[15]

The *mahā-mantra* is also referred to as the *pāraka-brahma-mahā-mantra.* Śrī Caitanya chanted this *mahā-mantra* and through the Goswāmīs he revealed an unparalleled understanding of its ramifications. People chant this mantra for everything from material gain to liberation from material existence to love of God, but no one has revealed its inner significance more than Śrī Caitanya. Through the Goswāmīs, Śrī Caitanya gave the world the highest conception of the name of Kṛṣṇa and the *mahā-mantra.* For Śrī Caitanya, Kṛṣṇa is the transcendental cowherder and, more, the lover of Rādhā. Rāma is another name of Kṛṣṇa himself, Ramaṇa, who gives pleasure to Rādhā. Hare is grammatically derived from *hṛ*, "to steal." Hari is Kṛṣṇa who takes away all of our possessions to demonstrate that it is to him alone that all things, ourselves included, belong. Yet Hare also indicates that lady who steals the heart of Hari. She is Rādhā, and in this mantra, she surrounds Kṛṣṇa on all sides.

The word *pāraka* can justifiably be viewed as a derivative of *pārayati*, to be qualified or competent. If we understand *pāraka* in this way, we can then ask where the *mahā-mantra*'s competence lies. The Goswāmīs and their followers will reply that it grants one the competence to conquer Kṛṣṇa, also known as *samartha*. Rūpa Goswāmī has identified the love of Rādhā as *samartha-rati*, and the implication of the word *pāraka-brahma-nāma* is that the *mahā-mantra* has been imbued with this love. Tasting this love in the context of chanting the *mahā-mantra*, Raghunātha Dāsa Goswāmī says:

> *O my greedy tongue!*
> *Don't you know that the name of Rādhā*
> *is like fresh new ambrosia and the name of Kṛṣṇa*

is like wonderful, sweet thick condensed milk?
Add the camphor scent of your attachment
and mix them together—and then drink,
drink eternally to your heart's content.[16]

Thus chanting the *mahā-mantra,* as received from the guru representing Śrī Caitanya's precepts, acquaints the disciple with the inner significance of the *rāsa-pañcādhyāya*, the supermost of Kṛṣṇa's *līlās,* in which the glory of Rādhā's love for Kṛṣṇa is central.

Chanting the *mahā-mantra* first cleanses the consciousness of all misgivings and material desires, thus affording liberation. After this is achieved, it begins to reveal its inner significance. Śrī Caitanya has said that the congregational chanting of the sacred name of Kṛṣṇa is the wife of knowledge, the beauty of the truth, and it thus acquaints the practitioner with the gopīs' love for Kṛṣṇa.[17] The esoteric mantras given to the disciple help him to take advantage of that which is within the *mahā-mantra* and enable him to perform ritualistic worship.

Ritualistic worship of the images of Rādhā and Kṛṣṇa enshrined in a temple or one's home requires invoking the esoteric mantras received from the guru.

A disciplined system of ritual worship plays an important role in the beginning stages of establishing a relationship with Kṛṣṇa. Such ritual is aesthetically pleasing and creates a spiritual atmosphere conducive to meditation.

Although ritualistic *bhakti* is a path unto itself culminating in reverential love of God, many of its practices are helpful if not essential in the culture of passionate love. To access the eternal drama through sacred literature, one must pass through evolutionary stages of practice. One must go step by step up the ladder of love, from initial faith to spontaneous love.

Rūpa Goswāmī has described the *adhikāra,* or eligibility, for treading the path of passionate love as *lobha*, greed. He mentions this in his *Bhakti-rasāmṛta-sindhu* after delineating *vaidhi-bhakti*, ritualistic devotion guided by scriptural injunctions. As opposed to *rāga*, which guides the practitioner by the force of its own passion, ritualistic *bhakti* is driven by reasoning and scriptural mandates. Although ritualistic *bhakti* is a separate path, Rūpa Goswāmī is concerned with it only as a support for *rāgānuga-bhakti*. Thus his discussion of ritualistic *bhakti* is not entirely divorced from that of *rāgānuga*.[18]

For although the path of passionate love is not motivated by scriptural prohibitions, in its dawning stages it derives support from ritualistic *bhakti*.[19]

The connection between ritualistic *bhakti* and passionate love is twofold in terms of the type of practitioner. One type of practitioner has a taste for love of Kṛṣṇa and the other does not. The path of passionate love can be trodden by either those in whom a taste for hearing and chanting about Kṛṣṇa has awakened (*jāta-ruci*) or by those who as yet have no such natural aptitude (*ajāta-ruci*). Those who are *jāta-ruci* have been advised by Jīva Goswāmī to follow the injunctions of ritualistic *bhakti* to set an example for those who are *ajāta-ruci*. He advises those who are *ajāta-ruci*, on the other hand, to follow the guidelines of ritualistic *bhakti* with a view to attaining a taste for love of Kṛṣṇa.[20]

The importance of ritualistic *bhakti* thus cannot be underestimated for those who choose the path of passionate love. At the same time, the two, passionate love and ritualistic devotion, seem diametrically opposed. One is the path of lawless passion, the other the path of law leading to a regulated passionless love of God.[21]

The general conception of love of God is steeped in awe and reverence. This type of love is the fruit of ritualistic *bhakti* when it is engaged in as a path unto itself. Ritualistic *bhakti* does not automatically lead to passionate love. It only assists in awakening *rāga* when it is engaged in as a support for the ideal of passionate love.

The word *vaidhi* is derived from *vidhi*, or "rules." Ritualistic *bhakti*, however, is not concerned with religious codes; it is concerned with the guidelines of *bhakti* itself. The value of religious codes lies in their giving rise to *bhakti*.[22] If after practicing the religious injunctions, one does not develop *bhakti*, one's time has been wasted.[23] Thus as *dharma*, or religious life, reaches its perfection when it culminates in *bhakti*, so ritualistic *bhakti* reaches its highest perfection when it is used as a means to develop passionate love.

The wisdom of ritualistic *bhakti* is deep. It is designed to redirect our nature from serving the dictates of the mind and senses in the name of enjoyment to serving Kṛṣṇa through the very same activities. The devotee on the path of ritualistic *bhakti* uses the senses in the service of Kṛṣṇa by hearing and chanting about Kṛṣṇa, tasting only food that has been first offered to Kṛṣṇa, smelling incense and flowers offered to Kṛṣṇa, touching and viewing the deity form of Kṛṣṇa, and so on.

Altogether, Rūpa Goswāmī has mentioned 64 practices of ritualistic *bhakti* in *Bhakti-rasāmṛta-sindhu*. Careful analysis of these practices reveals a very strict and consuming devotional life. One so engaged will be safe from the many distracting thoughts that arise in the mind and thus will stay on course for spiritual attainment.

Ritualistic *bhakti* gives support to those who as yet have no relish for the discussion of Kṛṣṇa *līlā*, a relish that on a regular basis may keep one awake the entire night, hearing and chanting about Kṛṣṇa. Those who have attained the state of relish or taste need no support or structure for their life of devotion. Their ongoing culture of love is driven by their acquired taste alone. Those who have not reached this stage, however, rely upon the structure of ritualistic *bhakti* to support their culture of love. Thus they embrace the majority of Rūpa Goswāmī's 64 devotional principles out of necessity, rather than to set an example for others. The difference between their embrace of these principles and that of those who tread the path of ritualistic *bhakti* is impulse. The impulse of those on the path of ritualistic *bhakti* is the principle or injunction itself. Perfect adherence to the injunctions is their desired goal, resulting in reverential love of God. The impulse of the practitioner of passionate love, on the other hand, is eagerness to attain that which the gopīs embody—an intimate relationship with Kṛṣṇa in which reverence is overridden by spontaneous, noncalculative love.

All of the devotional practices of ritualistic *bhakti* relative to the culture of passionate love are conducted in the *sādhaka-deha*, the external spiritualized body of the practitioner received at the time of initiation.[24] The *sādhaka-deha* is not a material body, nor is it a perfected spiritual body. It is a material body in transformation to a spiritualized material body. Just as in appearance a gold-plated box functions as a gold box, similarly the *sādhaka-deha* gradually becomes spiritualized and thus functions spiritually. From the time of his initiation, the practitioner's body begins to take on a spiritual quality. Proportionate to the extent that his senses and mind are spiritually engaged in hearing, chanting, serving, and meditating, and so on, the practitioner's body is spiritualized. To the extent that his senses are not engaged, his body remains material. When the practitioner reaches perfection, his *sādhaka-deha* is fully spiritualized. Evidence for this is found in the *Bhāgavatam*, wherein certain devotees are said to have achieved status in the *līlā* of Viṣṇu in their transformed practitioner bodies.[25] The body of the perfect practitioner is thus entombed at the time of his apparent death in a *samādhī-mandir*.

Along with the external practices performed in the *sādhaka-deha*, those on the path of passionate love engage in meditation upon their *siddha-deha*, an inner spiritual body. The *siddha-deha* is indicated in the Upaniṣads[26] and explained further in the *Śrīmad-Bhāgavatam*. Sage Nārada describes in his conversation with Vyāsa how he realized his perfected spiritual body.[27] The *siddha-deha* is not a perfected material body, but a spiritual one in every respect. The practitioner's perfected body is the body in which he eternally participates in Kṛṣṇa *līlā*. It is a body made up of Kṛṣṇa's internal potency, *svarūpa-śakti*.

The inner spiritual body is revealed to the disciple by the guru when the guru perceives the mature eagerness to receive it. Just as the inheritance of a youth may be withheld by his elders until his eagerness to spend it meets with a mature understanding of its value, the guru withholds this revelation until he sees mature eagerness in his disciple. Such eagerness is characterized by the practitioner's ability to meditate continually upon the *siddha-deha* while engaging externally in the practices of ritualistic *bhakti* relative to the culture of *rāgānuga-bhakti*. This generally occurs in the final stages of practicing life (*āsakti*).

Attempts to practice this type of meditation before inner purity is attained are often met with disappointment. They are usually forced and artificial, lending to imagination, as opposed to actually following in the wake of the spiritual feelings of the gopīs. In recent times, this happened on such a wide scale that some *ācāryas* suggested reform. Such reform involved placing even greater emphasis on chanting the *mahā-mantra* congregationally and, for the qualified practitioner, meditation (*ātmā dhyāna*) upon the *bhāva* of the gopī assistants of Rādhā as described in sacred literature.[28] In this case, conceptualization of the inner spiritual body is manifest through the spiritual practice itself, as opposed to being given by the guru at the time of a special initiation.

Internal cultivation of the *bhāva* described in the literature combined with external chanting of the *mahā-mantra* naturally gives rise to actual realization of one's eternal spiritual body due to the power of the sacred literature and the inconceivable potency of the sacred name of Kṛṣṇa.[29] This potent practice purifies the heart such that the practitioner is gradually and naturally drawn to inner contemplative life. Jīva Goswāmī has compared this inner purity of the heart to a *sphaṭika-maṇi*, or mirror. The soul, that is, must have the clarity of a mirror to reflect accurately the moods of the residents of Vṛndāvana whose attitude of love he wishes to emulate.

Jīva Goswāmī explains in his *Prīti-sandarbha* that there are unlimited spiritual forms in the domain of Kṛṣṇa. With each form, Kṛṣṇa enjoys a transcendental relationship. These forms exist eternally, even before the aspiring soul is aware of his particular form. Realization of one's form is the crown jewel of spiritual attainment. The form is awakened in accordance with the soul's particular ideal imbibed from his spiritual preceptor. Prior to the aspiring soul's realization of the spiritual body, it exists in an inactive state.

The *siddha-deha* is a spiritual/emotional (*bhāva*) body. For those who meditate upon the *rāsa-pañcadhyaya* as recommended by Śrī Caitanya, this body consists of the *bhāva* of one of Rādhā's maidservant friends. Although other gopīs also love Kṛṣṇa, Rādhā's love is primary. Thus Śrī Caitanya recommended that one follow the friends of Rādhā, thereby experiencing her love. In this regard, Śrī Caitanya directed all souls to Rūpa Goswāmī, who in his *siddha-deha* is Rūpa Mañjarī, a close friend of Rādhā and follower of her friend, Lalitā Sakhī. Practitioners desirous of attaining the zenith of aesthetic rapture follow the lead of Rūpa Mañjarī.[30]

Following Rūpa Mañjarī in the context of practice means to await and aspire for that time in eternity when Rūpa Mañjarī gives one engagement in the service of Rādhā. In aspiring to this, one's practice primarily involves developing attachment for hearing regularly about Rādhā and Kṛṣṇa and their associated servant friends, the *mañjarīs*. In this spiritual/emotional reality, the devotee aspires not to be a direct mistress of Kṛṣṇa, but an assistant of the *mañjarīs* in uniting Rādhā with Kṛṣṇa. In assisting the *mañjarīs*, the devotee experiences heightened aesthetic rapture equal to or greater than that of even Rādhā. This is so because their unswerving allegiance to Rādhā, Kṛṣṇa's true love, fully purchases Kṛṣṇa.[31] This we heard directly from Kṛṣṇa in *rāsa-pañcadhyāya*.

As we have seen, *rāsa-pañcadhyāya* is about Rādhā's love for Kṛṣṇa. This love is worshipped by the connoisseur of love himself, *rasa-rāja* Kṛṣṇa. Even Kṛṣṇa desires to experience this love, and revealing this desire as he does in *rāsa-pañcadhyāya*, he makes known to all souls their highest prospect in the pursuit of the ultimate truth.

The Goswāmīs have left a wealth of literature that explains the emotions of Rādhā's maidservants, such as Śrī Rūpa Mañjarī, in the context of descriptions of Kṛṣṇa's *līlās*. Careful study of these texts in the association of advanced practitioners and perfected devotees, combined with regular chanting of Kṛṣṇa's sacred names, makes for a spiritual practice that is itself sublime, leading to passionate love in Kṛṣṇa *līlā*.

Every aspect of Kṛṣṇa's *līlā* is eternal, just as with the movements of the sun every moment of time is ever manifest. The advanced practitioner has so absorbed his mind in Kṛṣṇa that he is meditating upon Kṛṣṇa all day and night. He divides the day into eight periods (*aṣṭa-kāla*). During each of these periods, he internally envisions the corresponding *līlās* of Kṛṣṇa.

The *Bhāgavatam*, while revealing the basic story of Kṛṣṇa *līlā*, focuses primarily on the *bhāva* that is the essence of Kṛṣṇa's world of love. In the writings of the Goswāmīs, further details of the eternal drama are revealed. Kṛṣṇadāsa Kavirāja Goswāmī wrote *Govinda-līlāmṛta*, in which he described an eternal day in the life of Rādhā and Kṛṣṇa. The text, while describing only one typical day of Kṛṣṇa, consists of more than 2,300 verses. Meditation upon this extensive poem is common among advanced practitioners today. Other than the spiritual vision of its author, Kavirāja Goswāmī's poem is based upon an 11-stanza poetic description of Kṛṣṇa's daily *līlā* attributed to Rūpa Goswāmī. Rūpa Goswāmī's stanzas are in turn based upon the account of Kṛṣṇa's typical day related in the *Padma Purāṇa*. As in our everyday lives there are fixed times for eating, resting, and recreation, so also in the daily *līlā* of Kṛṣṇa.

The structure of Kṛṣṇa's day thus serves as an excellent meditative focus for the advanced practitioner throughout his day. Rather than constituting a world-denying life, such meditation on Kṛṣṇa *līlā* throughout the day overflows into this world bringing new meaning into everyday life. In relation to *rāsa-līlā* in particular, it gives sacred meaning to the erotic tendency within humanity.

In the *aṣṭa-kāla* meditation, Rādhā and Kṛṣṇa perform their *rāsa-līlā* every night. After the conclusion of the *rāsa-līlā,* Rādhā and Kṛṣṇa rest in the forest bowers on a bed of flowers. One and one-half hours before sunrise, they are awakened by their servant friends. As they realize that they must return to their homes before they are discovered by their elders, their anguish in separation knows no bounds. This separation known as *vipralambha* is experienced by their intimate friends as well. The advanced practitioner meditating on this *līlā* also experiences Rādhā's feeling of separation from Kṛṣṇa, an emotional experience that intensifies the practitioner's love for the divine couple. The following verse from Viśvanātha Cakravartī Ṭhākura's *Kṛṣṇa-bhāvanāmṛta* serves as an example of the poetic meditation upon the eightfold daily *līlā* of Rādhā and Kṛṣṇa.

"As dawn approached, Rādhā and Kṛṣṇa went arm in arm from their forest cottage, about to step into the cow pasture on their way home. At that time, Śyāmasundara, the beautiful dark boy, fearing the imminent appearance of the sun and the arrival of Rādhā's mother-in-law, Jaṭilā, suddenly removed Rādhā's arm from his shoulder. It was as though the joy of their union ended at the junction of the forest and the pasture, where the kingdom of anxiety began. Rādhā had obtained a great treasure in the form of Kṛṣṇa's arm, with the help of the general of her eagerness. Yet now, as they arrived at the edge of Vraja, a more powerful soldier, doubt, had defeated this general and forcefully removed her treasured possession. When the doubts that threatened Rādhā and Kṛṣṇa refused to allow them to continue on to their homes in union, their pain in separation caused their friends who were leading the way to sigh and break out in tears."[32]

In the example above, the practitioner identifies with the dominant emotion *(sthāyī-bhāva)* of conjugal love as experienced by Rādhā and Kṛṣṇa's servant friends *(tad-bhavecchātmikā)*.[33] The object of love *(viṣaya-ālambana-vibhāva)* is Rādhā and Kṛṣṇa, and the shelter of that love *(āśraya-ālambana-vibhāva)* is Rādhā and Kṛṣṇa's servant friends, who become the practitioner's role models. The stimulus *(uddīpana-vibhava)* is the tearful look on the faces of Rādhā and Kṛṣṇa. The ensuant ecstasies *(anubhāvas)* are the long sighs of the *mañjarīs*. The involuntary ecstasies *(sattvika-bhāvas)* are shedding tears and discoloration of the face. The auxiliary emotions *(vyabhicāri-bhāvas)* are depression, anxiety, and fever.

Hearing or meditating upon the *niśānta-līlā* (end of night) described in the above verse, the practitioner, following in the mood of Rūpa Goswāmī, experiences Rādhā's separation from Kṛṣṇa vicariously. He imbibes the mood of one of Rādhā's maidservant friends in leading the divine couple home. As Rādhā's separation is great, more so is that of her friends. The advanced practitioner, by identifying with the elements of *rasa* contained in the poetry, experiences the dominant emotion along with the other ingredients of aesthetic rapture. Rūpa Goswāmī calls this method of vicarious experience *sādhāraṇī-karaṇa*.[34]

In meditating upon *rāsa-līlā*, followers of Rūpa Goswāmī aspire to assist the divine couple. As seen in the example above, Rādhā and Kṛṣṇa are the object of love (*viṣaya-ālambana-vibhāva*). The *mañjarī* handmaidens of Rādhā are the ideal to follow, the embodiment of that love (*āśraya-ālambana-vibhāva*). The object and embodiment of love in the eternal drama of passionate love are Rādhā-Kṛṣṇa and Rādhā's handmaidens, respectively. The excitants of that love (*uddīpana-vibhāvas*) are Rādhā and Kṛṣṇa's qualities, names, activities, dress, related items, and general impetuses for romantic sentiments. The word *vibhāva* is derived from the Sanskrit verb *vi-bhū*, the root of which means to grow, to flourish, or to become glorious. Thus the *vibhāvas* cause one's acquired dominant emotion (*sthāyi-bhāva*) to flourish into the glory of *rasānanda*.

Internal visualization of Rādhā and Kṛṣṇa has been described by advanced devotees. Static meditation is called *mantra-mayī* and dynamic visualization is known as *svārasikī*. In *mantra-mayī* visualization, the practitioner meditates upon a particular pose of Kṛṣṇa or a scene from his pastimes as found in a mantra from sacred literature or one given by the guru. The most common form of *mantra-mayī* meditation focuses on the Yoga-pīṭha, in which Rādhā and Kṛṣṇa are surrounded by the chief *sakhīs* and *mañjarīs* and receive ritualistic worship such as that which is given in the *ārati* ceremony. Meditation on the *rāsa-līlā* is an example of *svārasikī*. Ability to perform this meditation develops out of *mantra-mayī* visualization. If *mantra-mayī* were compared to a lake, *svārasikī* would be compared to thousands of streams that flow from it.

Through *svārasikī* visualization, the practitioner in effect "creates his own reality" within ultimate reality, his visualization being bound only by the parameters of *rasa-tattva* that govern this spiritual world. The mental technique for such visualization is outwardly similar to that found in sects of Tantric Buddhism or Loyola's "spiritual exercises," but the inner dynamics that call for purity of consciousness as a prerequisite differentiate it from these traditions. Furthermore, visualization as found in other traditions represents an approximation of *mantra-mayī*, and there is no real parallel practice of *svārasikī*.

In *mantra-mayī* visualization, the divine couple are meditated upon as they appear at the time of the *rāsa-*

līlā. Kṛṣṇa is 15 years, 9 months, and 7 1/2 days old. He is a *dhīra-lalita* hero, one who is both sober and playful. He has 32 auspicious bodily characteristics and 64 principal qualities. He plays a flute and wears a garland of forest flowers extending to his knees. He is decorated with jewels, and his body is smeared with various unguents. He is the embodiment of romantic attraction. Before his *rāsa-līlā,* all of these qualities are not fully manifest. They manifest in connection with Rādhā's love.

Rādhā stands to his left. Her bodily hue is golden, like that of the celebrated *campaka* flower sprinkled with saffron. Its color is the same as Kṛṣṇa's dress. Rādhā wears a garment the color of the raincloud-like complexion of Kṛṣṇa. Her body has the scent of a lotus flower. Her eyes are black and expanded like a fully blossomed lotus. She has 25 principal qualities and a temperamental romantic disposition.

Rūpa Goswāmī has left us the following visualization of the divine couple: "I meditate on the forms of Śrī Śrī Rādhā and Kṛṣṇa as their bewitching eyes drink in each other's beauty with mutual glances of intense affection. They have their trembling arms wrapped around one another and are wearing gold and black garments, respectively. They are aglow with their intense eagerness for erotic pastimes."[35]

Rādhā's maidservant friends, who serve as the ideal to follow, are also described by the Goswāmīs. They have all of the qualities of Rādhā, and are thus equally competent to satisfy Kṛṣṇa. They have these qualities by way of identification with Rādhā. Because their super-excellent *bhāva* is derived thus *(tad-bhāva)*, they will never directly consort with Kṛṣṇa. Their paramour love is a product of identifying wholly with Rādhā in service to her. An example of their service during the *rāsa-līlā* is found in *Prārthanāmṛta-taraṅginī* in a song attributed to Vaiṣṇava dasa: "O daughter of King Vṛṣabhānu! Rādhe! When will your dear handmaiden Śrī Guṇa Mañjarī take me into her fold? After you two are exhausted from dancing in *rāsa-līlā* and are sitting together on a raised platform to rest, dizzy and perspiring, then by her mercy, receiving her hinting glance, I along with Rati-mañjarī will come and fan you with yak-tail whisks. I will wash and dry your faces and feet, and Rūpa-mañjarī will give me pan to place in your mouths. By my service your fatigue will soon be removed, and you will feel comfortable and relaxed. Vaiṣṇava dasa prays that this desire be fulfilled, for what could be worse than its non-fulfillment?"

Meditating on Kṛṣṇa *līlā* from the perspective of one's inner spiritual body, the practitioner sometimes experiences himself to be part of the *līlā* and sometimes sees himself as a practitioner, aware of his practitioner's body. When he experiences himself as part of the *līlā*, his meditation becomes his reality. He no longer sees himself as a viewer of the eternal drama; the emotions of the role model he follows become his own.

From simple remembrance of Kṛṣṇa *(smaraṇam)*, the practitioner moves to consciously removing any other thoughts, practicing concentration *(dhāraṇam)*, and then meditating *(dhyānam)*. It is at the stage of *dhyānam* that he can effectively envision the eternal daily *līlā* of Kṛṣṇa, become fixed in that meditation *(dhruvānusmṛti)*, and from there enter into it in *samādhi*, or trance of love. The advanced practitioner performs this meditation in the midst of daily activities involving his outer *sādhaka-deha*, visualizing what Rādhā and Kṛṣṇa are doing in their day from the perspective of his own aspired for role in his *siddha-deha*.[36]

The mature practitioner enters the eternal drama of Rādhā-Kṛṣṇa while reading, hearing, or remembering the passages of *rāsa-pañcādhyāya* or other similar literature. Kṛṣṇa has been called *uttama-śloka*, the perfection of verse. Such is the verse of the *Bhāgavatam* and the subsequent literature of the Goswāmīs. It is poetry that is reality, through which the connoisseur of *rasa* forgets his practitioner's body and the entire material world of falsity to live within the pages of the literature.

It may be difficult to conceive of poetry as reality, for in poetry one can do and see that which one cannot in the so-called "real" world of our sense experience. Yet *Śrīmad-Bhāgavatam* is not merely poetry. It is also a book of *siddhānta*, or conclusive knowledge, the ripened fruit of the wish-fulfilling tree known as the Vedas.[37]

From the Vedas one can get all knowledge. *Śrīmad-Bhāgavatam* represents the utmost knowledge one can get from this tree, the highest aspiration of the soul. Knowledge is as valuable as that which it affords us the capacity to do. All action requires some knowledge. That knowledge which affords us the capacity to love the Absolute is the highest knowledge. That love is a prospect so high that God himself bows to it. Its attainment fully satisfies the Absolute. While most are concerned with being satisfied by the Absolute, *Śrīmad-Bhāgavatam* proposes the opposite: a path whose goal is to comprehensively satisfy the Absolute. This satisfaction of the Absolute is possible through the utter selflessness of the path of passionate love.[38]

Absolute love is the ideal of the *Bhāgavatam*, the fruit of the highest knowledge. Its poetry is a description of the land of love, wherein all things are possible. If truth is love and beauty, it is reasonable that it be represented in poetry, wherein all things are possible. In poetry, land can turn into water and water into land, as it does in the *Bhāgavatam* when Kṛṣṇa plays his flute. Love resolves all contradictions, for in love our lover's faults become ornaments.

While meditating upon the divine poetry of *Śrīmad-Bhāgavatam*, the practitioner becomes increasingly absorbed, identifying the various constituents of *rasa* therein, nourishing his particular dominant emotion. Thus the verses come to life for the practitioner, and at the perfectional stage he experiences divine *rasa*.

Imbibing the spiritual emotions embodied in his ideal within the text, the practitioner's soul lives in that transcendent emotional reality.

The neophyte practitioner sometimes experiences a shadow or reflection of the eternal emotions of the *bhāva* he pursues. The advanced practitioner enters into *bhāva-bhakti*, which is the sprouting (*premāṅkura*) of the tree of *prema-bhakti*. He experiences a ray of the sun of *prema* under the influence of the internal spiritual energy of Kṛṣṇa.[39] Finally, he realizes *prema*, pure love of Kṛṣṇa. Not caring for anything other than the intensification of *prema*, he sometimes appears as if mad. His behavior can be as bewildering as the beauty of Kṛṣṇa *līlā* itself. It is said that Kṛṣṇa *prema* on the outside appears to be like poison, while on the inside it is ecstatic and beautiful. This is its wonderful and mysterious characteristic,[40] one that is just the opposite of the characteristic of material life. While material life looks appealing on the outside, it is rotten at the core.

As the gopīs cried in separation from Kṛṣṇa, they experienced the highest inner joy. Śrī Caitanya in the mood of Rādhā exhibited extraordinary bodily symptoms of ecstasy that would be disconcerting for the uninformed. His feelings of separation from Kṛṣṇa in the ecstasy of Śrī Rādhā teach us that union in love with Kṛṣṇa is possible through intense yearning. His transformations of ecstasy also teach us that the practitioner's present body, the *sādhaka-deha*, cannot contain the intensification of *prema*.[41]

Developments that constitute intensification of *prema* are part of the gradual evolution to spiritual perfection in passionate love. If these developmental stages are not to be experienced in the practitioner's earthly body, the question arises as to where and in what form the practitioner will culture them. He cannot do so in the eternally unmanifest *līlā* of Kṛṣṇa, for that realm is not for practitioners. Therefore, the practitioner after attaining *prema* in his present body must take another birth. He takes birth in the material world wherever Kṛṣṇa is manifesting his eternal *līlā*. This *līlā*, which manifest five thousand years ago in India, is what is described in the *Bhāgavatam*. It is always manifest somewhere in the material world in one of innumerable universes. This manifest *līlā* has both transcendental characteristics and phenomenal ones. The practitioner takes birth from the womb of a gopī and meets

Kṛṣṇa's eternally liberated gopī associates. The practitioner must take birth in conformity with the human-like nature of the eternal *līlā*. In that *līlā*, the soul experiences an intensification of *prema* relative to his particular spiritual body.[42] This spiritual body is constituted of the *bhāva* he has meditated upon in his previous life. From the manifest *līlā*, the perfect devotee is then transferred to the unmanifest *līlā* and thus to perfection, the culmination of the path of passionate love.

Passionate love of Kṛṣṇa is truth that is beautiful and bewildering. To embark upon it requires only that we cherish as our ideal the depths of the ocean of love of Kṛṣṇa. This is so because it is a person's ideal that he will become. It is the generous opinion of Śrī Caitanya that we should judge a person not by his past, nor even by the limits of his present. We should judge him by his ideal, for that he will become. We may not be prepared to adopt the aforementioned lifestyle, which constitutes the formal path of passionate love, yet if we are attracted to the ideal, we have come a long way toward realizing the truth that is beautiful. Merely cherishing this ideal amounts to a powerful spiritual practice. Śrī Jīva Goswāmī has written in his

Bhakti-sandarbha: "There is not even any real need for great effort in spiritual practice, for if one simply believes with all sincerity that he is the servant of Kṛṣṇa, that sense of spiritual identification will itself eventually give him all perfection."[43] Ṭhākura Bhaktivinoda also offers encouraging words in his *Śrī Caitanya-śikśāmṛta*. He tells us that the mere temptation to pursue the ideal of the Vraja-gopīs has such a spiritually powerful effect that it minimizes the effectiveness of adherence to ritualistic *bhakti*, what to speak of any other process.

As leaves fall naturally from the tree when the season changes from summer to fall, so that which impedes us from practicing the path of passionate love at present will fall away in due course. In our material lives, we inevitably become disenchanted with that for which we have striven. If that disenchantment is met with the inner ideal of passionate love of Kṛṣṇa, one day we will roam the cow pastures and forests along the banks of the Yamunā, answering to the clarion call of Kṛṣṇa's sweet flute.

O Mukunda, giver of liberation!
Who in the world is there with the courage

to pray for the gift of sacred passionate love,
of which the slightest manifestation
when brushing against the minds of the great sages
makes them forget the happiness of liberation?

My prayer therefore to you is this:
that I should desire for such love,
and that this desire should increase forever,
in this world, birth after birth.[44]

Abbreviations

Bg.	*Bhagavad-gītā*
Bhs.	*Bhakti-sandarbha*
Brs.	*Bhakti-rasāmṛta-sindhu*
Bs.	*Brahma-saṁhitā*
Bṛ. U.	*Bṛhad-āraṇyaka Upaniṣad*
Cc.	*Caitanya-caritāmṛta*
Ch. U.	*Chāndogya Upaniṣad*
GC.	*Gopāla Campū*
Gt. U.	*Gopāla-tāpanīya Upaniṣad*
K. U.	*Kena Upaniṣad*
Ks. U.	*Kalisantarana Upaniṣad*
M. U.	*Muṇḍaka Upaniṣad*
P. P.	*Padma Purāṇa*
Ṛ. V.	*Ṛg Veda*
SB.	*Śrīmad-Bhāgavatam*
Tai. U.	*Taittirīya Upaniṣad*
UN.	*Ujjvala-nīlamaṇi*
V. P.	*Viṣṇu Purāṇa*
Vs.	*Vedānta-sūtra*

Notes

PREFACE

1. *Vidagdha-mādhava* 1.2, also cited in Cc. Ādi 1.3.

INTRODUCTION

1. Prasada, Dr. S.S., *Bhagavata Purana: A Literary Study* (New Delhi: Capital Publishing House, 1984), p. 296.
2. Swami, A. C. Bhaktivedanta, *Kṛṣṇa: The Supreme Personality of Godhead* (Bhaktivedanta Book Trust, Los Angeles, 1970)

CHAPTER ONE

1. (Bṛ. U. 3.1) This aphorism is often cited by *advaitins* (monists) to establish that ultimate reality, Brahman, is devoid of qualities, form, activity, etc. I cite it here in terms of this understanding. Devotional Vedānta, however, understands it to indicate that the Absolute is "not this," or more than that which we can perceive with our senses. Such devotional explanations of the Upaniṣads are based on Baladeva Vidyābhūṣaṇa's commentary on *Vedānta-sūtra, Govinda-bhāṣya.* In all subsequent references to the Upaniṣads' statements analyzed in the *Vedānta-sūtras,* it is Baladeva's understanding of them that I refer to.
2. *īkṣater nāśabdam,* "Brahman is not such that it cannot be described by speech [*na aśabdam*], for it is seen [*īkṣateḥ*] that it is described [in the Upaniṣads, etc.]." (Vs. 1.1.6) The idea here is that the Absolute is not indescribable, which would render speech and sound relative and the Upaniṣads' advocacy suicidal. The Absolute is that about which one can never tire of speaking. It is infinitely filled with sound, as it is full in touch, form, taste, and fragrance.
3. *brahma satyaṁ jagat mithyā.* This is the famous state-

ment of Śaṅkara. It should be made clear that devotional Vedānta disagrees entirely with Śaṅkara's intended meaning. For Śaṅkara, the world is false, like a rope perceived as a snake. Devotional Vedāntists, however, acknowledge the phenomenal world as real (*māyā-śakti*) and only its effect upon the individual souls as false. The effect is a transformation of the energy of the Absolute.

4. *raso vai saḥ rasaṁ hy evāyaṁ labdhvānandī bhavati*, "*Rasa* is Brahman. Upon attaining Brahman, one experiences *rasa*." (Tai. U. 2.7)

5. If we consider, as we should, that Vedānta is in concert with the notion of the "great chain of being" and acknowledge a hierarchical, ontological order, beginning on the low end with matter and culminating in consciousness, Ken Wilber's statement is telling: "[Acknowledgment of this notion of reality is] so overwhelmingly wide–spread . . . that it is either the single greatest intellectual error ever to appear in humankind's history—an error so colossally widespread as to literally stagger the mind—or it is the single most accurate reflection of reality yet to appear." Ken Wilber, "The Great Chain of Being," *Journal of Humanistic Psychology*, Vol. 33, No. 3 (1993), p. 53.

6. Will Durant, *The Pleasures of Philosophy* (New York: Simon & Schuster, 1963), p. 203.

7. Abraham H. Maslow, *Toward a Psychology of Being* (New York: Van Nost and Peinhold Co., 1968), p. 73.

8. Abhinavagupta's religious orientation was Kāśmirī Śaivism, yet he may also have been influenced by *advaita-vedānta*. Certainly Bhaṭṭa Nyāyaka before him and Mammaṭa Bhaṭṭa after him were influenced by *advaita-vedānta*, and both of them have made this comparison between the experience of secular *rasa* and ultimate reality. Abhinavagupta entertained the idea but seems uncommitted to it.

9. *apūrvatad eva hi tat-pradhānatvāt/ prakāśavac ca avaiyarthyat/*

āha ca tanmātram/ darśayati ca atho api smaryate/
(Vs. 3.2.14–17)

10. *oṁ sat cid ānanda rūpāya kṛṣṇāyā kliṣṭhakāriṇe*
(Gt. U., *pūrva* 1.1)

11. *sat-puṇḍarīka nayanaṁ meghābhaṁ vaidyutāmbaraṁ dvibhujaṁ jnāna-mudrāḍhyaṁ vanamālinam nam īśvaram//*
(Gt. U., *pūrva* 1.12)

12. The Dāmodara and Brahmā-vimohana *līlās* illustrate this point in SB. 10.9 and SB. 10.14, respectively.

13. This is an excerpt from *Lectures on Divine Humanity*, a series of talks given by Solovyov in St. Petersburg between 1878 and 1881. His lectures were attended by the likes of Tolstoy and Dostoyevsky. The lecture quoted was published in *Lapis*, Summer 1995.

14. Kṛṣṇa, as the primal Godhead, contains within himself all forms of Godhead, including Viṣṇu and his innumerable incarnations, all of which are expressions of his multidimensional personality. These various incarnations appear to reciprocate with the pure love of different devotees. In this book, we are concerned only with Kṛṣṇa in his fullest expression as the charming lover of the gopīs.

15. *ānandamayo 'bhyāsāt*, "The Absolute is joy, for repeatedly [throughout the Upaniṣads] it is described as such." (Vs. 1.1.12)

16. This poem is of unknown origin. It was translated by Jan Brzezinski. It and other translations by Brzezinski cited throughout are from his unpublished manuscripts of Jiva Goswāmī's *Gopāla Campū* and Kuñjabihārī Dāsa's *Mañjarī-svarūpa-nirūpaṇa*.

17. Kṛṣṇa has three principal energies: internal (*svarūpa śakti*), marginal (*taṭastha śakti*), and external (*māyā śakti*). Rādhā represents the essence of the internal energy. Bound souls are particles of the marginal energy, and matter is a manifestation of the external energy.

18. *lokavat tu līlā-kaivalyam*, "The Absolute creates the phenomenal world out of sport, as do worldly beings [sometimes] act [in sport out of joy]." (Vs. 2.1.33)

19. SB. 10.33.36

20. *akhila-rasāmṛta mūrti* (Brs. 1.1.1)

21. Laws of Heracleitus LXXIX

22. *lokavat tu līlā-kaivalyam* (Vs. 2.1.33)

23. Bg. 3.22

24. See Viśvanātha's commentary on Kavi Karṇapura's *Alaṅkāra Kaustubha* (5.16).

25. Brs. 2.5.46

26. Bharata also mentions involuntary emotions (*sāttvika-bhāvas*) in his secular theory. They are eight in number: perspiration, horripilation, tears, choking of the voice, becoming stunned, changing colors, trembling, and fainting.

27. Bṛ. Up. (2.4.5) offers a lengthy explanation of the concept that love is based on consciousness, the soul, and ultimately the Supreme Soul. SB. 10.14.54–55 also teaches this at the philosophical conclusion of the *Brahmā-vimohana-līlā*, where Kṛṣṇa is ultimately pointed to as the source of love. One loves oneself only because the self is derived from Kṛṣṇa, just as one loves one's body, family, country, etc., only because they are extensions of the self.

28. *artho' yam brahma-sūtrāṇām* . . . This verse does not appear in any current manuscript of the *Garuḍa Purāṇa*, but it is cited in the *Tattva-sandarbha* of Jīva Goswāmī, as well as in the *Caitanya-caritāmṛta*, both of which attribute it to the *Garuḍa Purāṇa*. The verse was also cited by Mādhvācārya.

29. P. P., *uttara-khaṇḍa* 191.15

30. *śruti-sāram ekam* (SB. 1.2.3), *sarva-vedānta-sāraṁ hi* . . . (SB. 12.13.12)

31. SB. 1.1.3

32. This title has come to mean one who has mastered (*swāmī*) his senses (*go*). I use the term throughout this book

to refer to highly realized souls in the Gauḍīya tradition.

33. This is first mentioned in Brs. 2.5.128. Therein, Rūpa Goswāmī mentions that although Kṛṣṇa is the object of love, sometimes his friend also becomes that object along with him. Jīva Goswāmī's commentary on Rūpa Goswāmī's verse identifies this friend as Rādhā. The Goswāmīs have directed their love to Rādhā more than Kṛṣṇa, and thus they experience her ecstasy, which even Kṛṣṇa longs to taste.

34. Support for this idea is found in Bg. 18.64. Although Viśvanātha Cakravartī Ṭhākura has explained the concluding verse of Śukadeva Goswāmī's description of Rādhā-Kṛṣṇa's *rāsa līlā* (SB. 10.33.39) such that it indicates one need not be liberated to cultivate the highest variety of *bhakti-rasa*, all the Goswāmīs agree that *rasa* is ultimately a post-liberated experience.

35. SB. 10.14.3

36. According to the *Bhāgavatam*, Cupid's body was burnt to ashes by the anger of Śiva, and thus he is known as *anaṅga*, "without limbs." (SB. 10.55.1) While Śiva partially defeats Cupid by destroying his body, Kṛṣṇa defeats Cupid and enlists him in his service.

37. The *kāma gāyatrī* invoked by Gauḍīya Vedāntins is referred to here: *klīṁ kāmadevāya vidmahe puṣpabāṇāya dhīmahi tan no 'naṅgaḥ pracodayāt.* Here, *kāmadevāya* refers to Madana-mohana, the deity of Kṛṣṇa that represents *mantra-dīkṣā* (initiation), which is a function of *sambandha-jñāna*, or knowledge of one's relationship with Kṛṣṇa as an eternal servant. *Puṣpabāṇāya* refers to the deity of Kṛṣṇa known as Govinda, who represents the means *(abhidheya)* of awakening love of God. *Anaṅgaḥ* refers to Gopinātha, the deity of Kṛṣṇa that represents the goal *(prayojana)* of love of Kṛṣṇa, especially the love of the gopīs. This *kāma gāyatrī* is received at the time of initiation and is considered to represent the fifth note of Kṛṣṇa's flute.

38. Bound souls can also enter the *rāsa-līlā* by following in the footsteps of the gopīs. This is the path of passionate love.

39. *Mādhava* means *spring*. It is one of Kṛṣṇa's innumerable names.

40. I have drawn from Vallabha's insights only when they follow in the spirit of the Goswāmīs. It must be noted that Rūpa Goswāmī has acknowledged considerable similarity between his teaching in *Bhakti-rasāmṛta-sindhu* and that of Vallabhācārya. At the end of Rūpa Goswāmī's two sections on *sādhana-bhakti*, he wrote favorably about Vallabha's corresponding doctrines of *sādhana*.

CHAPTER TWO

1. (Cc. Madhya 21.137–143) Thus spoke Śrī Caitanya in the madness of Rādhā's love for Kṛṣṇa. Trans. by Jan Brzezinski.

2. *janma-ādi asya yataḥ*, "Brahman is he from whom the world manifests, and by whom it is maintained and destroyed." (Vs. 1.1.1)

3. *rasaṁ evāyaṁ labdhvānandī bhavati* (Tai. U. 2.7)

4. *upasthite' tas tad-vacanāt*, "The Absolute has erotic sentiment in connection with his *śakti*, as the *śruti* states." (Vs. 3.3.42). Gt. U. (*Uttar* 22) is referred to herein. "He who through lust desires the objects of desire is known as *kāmī*. He who has no lust yet desires objects [out of the fullness of love] is known as *akāmī*." Here the word *akāma* does not mean "without desire," but "something like *kāma*, yet not *kāma*." When lust is transformed into love, it is called *akāma*. Because the Absolute's object of love is his own *śakti*, his joy is not dependent upon anything other than himself. Thus his joy is like that of one looking in the mirror, for his *śakti* reveals him even to himself.

5. SB. 10.22.27

6. *tat tu samanvayāt* (Vs. 1.1.4)

7. Such is the case for the gopīs who became perfect through spiritual practice. The Goswāmīs have categorized the gopīs into two principal groups: those who are eternally perfect (*nitya-siddha*) and those who became perfect through spiritual practice (*sādhana-siddha*). The *sādhana-siddha* gopīs are further subdivided into those who became perfect along with others in a group and those who were not in a group. Those who came in a group are further divided into the *ṛṣis* of Daṇḍaka forest and the Upaniṣads. The *deva-kanyās*, daughters of the demigods, who are mentioned elsewhere, are explained in *Ujjvala-nīlamaṇī* as partial expansions of the *nitya-siddha* gopīs.

8. GC., *pūrva* 23.19. Trans. by Jan Brzezinski.

9. *Anurāga* is an intensified state of *prema* experienced primarily by the gopīs. In this experience, the gopīs perceive Kṛṣṇa to be everfresh, appearing newer and newer even though they have always known him. Here, Kṛṣṇa desires to experience *anurāga* with the gopīs. *Rāga* is also a musical expression.

10. See SB. 10.21 and GC., *pūrva* 18.

11. *Padma Purāṇa, sṛṣti khaṇḍa* and UN. 3.46.

12. This is an example of the *anubhāva* of *vibhrama*, bewilderment.

13. Viśvānatha Cakravartī Ṭhākura cites SB. 10.47.38–39 to establish that the gopīs who were stopped from meeting Kṛṣṇa did not physically die but acquired spiritual bodies and continued to participate in Kṛṣṇa's earthly *līlā*. The gopīs mentioned in these verses who had "their memories revived" were those gopīs who had been initially stopped from meeting Kṛṣṇa.

14. Orthodox Christians hold that Christ is fully God and fully man. As man, he underwent the experience of

suffering and death, through which he atoned for man's sins, something that could only be done by God incarnate. In Gauḍīya Vaiṣṇava theology, Kṛṣṇa is fully God and fully human, but not in the sense that he undergoes material suffering. The fullness of Kṛṣṇa's humanity is expressed when he falls in love. This, however, is also divine, for in doing so he elevates humans to divine life. Although Kṛṣṇa is fully God and fully human, he is human only in the sense that his life is humanlike. The difference can be most clearly seen in the contrast between the word *avatāra* (one who descends) and incarnation (one who comes in the flesh).

15. *Gopāla-tāpanīya Upaniṣad* relates the story of the gopīs' desire to cross the Yamunā. Upon being asked by the gopīs to help them cross the Yamunā, Kṛṣṇa told them to say "Kṛṣṇa is a *brahmacārī* (celibate)," and in this way the river would allow them to cross. Confused because of their dalliances with him the previous night, yet obedient and ever-faithful, they uttered these words and the waves of the Yamunā parted. The purport of this story is that a great soul can be engaged in what appears to be sense gratification while in fact be free from any mundane influence because he engages in such activity for the pleasure of the Absolute.

16. The sons of the gopīs were not theirs through childbirth. It is the village custom for women to take care of each other's children.

17. These six opulences are wealth, strength, beauty, fame, knowledge, and renunciation. (V.P. 6.5.47)

18. SB. 5.18.21

19. This is an example of the *vyabhicārī-bhāva* of *cintā*, anxiety, symptoms of which are drawing lines on the ground, breathing deeply, lowering one's head, etc.

20. This is an example of the *sāttvika-bhāva*, or involuntary expression, of *svara-bheda*, faltering of the voice.

21. SB. 1.3.28

22. SB. 5.1.13

23. Bg. 7.18

24. Lakṣmī is the goddess of fortune, the wife of Nārāyaṇa. According to the Purāṇas, although she has a permanent position on the chest of Nārāyaṇa, she nonetheless desired to dwell at the feet of Kṛṣṇa, who is the source of Nārāyaṇa.

25. SB. 10.8.19

26. Bg. 18.66

27. This poem is based on GC., *pūrva* 23.13.

28. *pūrva-vikalpaḥ prakaraṇāt syāt kriyā mānasavat,* "This *so' ham* is a form of that previously mentioned *(bhakti),* because of the context [in which it appears in the Upaniṣads], just as worship, meditation, and so on [are forms of *bhakti*]." (Vs. 3.3.46) This *sūtra* explains the statement in *Gopāla-tāpanīya Upaniṣad*, wherein it is recommended that one meditate, "I am he; I am Gopāla [Kṛṣṇa]." Although this seems at first to indicate identity between the soul and Brahman in all respects, understood in the context of the entire Upaniṣad it is apparent that this is not the spirit of the text. Rather it is a particular form of *bhakti*. In UN. 11.28–30, Rūpa Goswāmī identifies it as the *anubhāva* called *līlā*, which he understands to mean "imitation of the beloved."

29. This is the *vyabhicārī-bhāva* known as *unmāda*, madness.

30. These *līlās* are described in detail in the *Bhāgavatam*'s eighth and third cantos, respectively. The Varāha incarnation is said to be the husband of Bhūmi devī, the earth goddess.

31. All of these *līlās* are recorded in early chapters of the tenth canto of the *Bhāgavatam*.

32. This is the sequence of events with regard to the speech of different gopīs as per Bhaktivinoda Ṭhākura's *Bhāgavata-arka-marīci-nimāla*. Other Goswāmīs have attributed the speech in which Rādhā is praised as the best worshipper of Kṛṣṇa (*anayārādhito nūnam,* SB. 10.30.28) to gopīs of Rādhā's

group. The idea that it was Rādhā's friends who spoke in praise of her seems more appropriate in consideration of sentiment. They also must have known the footprint of Rādhā. On the other hand, attributing this speech to Candrāvalī certainly brings out the glory of Śrī Rādhā in no uncertain terms, for she is Rādhā's chief competitor. If even Candrāvalī says Rādhā's love is best, who can disagree?

33. Normally this is the influence of the *vyabhicārī-bhāva* of *garva*.

34. This is an instance of *premavaicittya* in *adhirūḍha-madana mahābhāva*, in which, according to Rūpa Goswāmī's *Ujjvala-nīlamaṇi,* the bewildered beloved experiences separation from her lover even in his presence.

35. GC., *pūrva* 24.81. Trans. by Jan Brzezinski.

36. The description regarding Rādhā's compassion for the other gopīs, etc. is based on Viśvanātha Cakravartī Ṭhākura's *Prema-sampuṭikā (The Love-Locket),* wherein, through the pen of Viśvanātha, Rādhā tells her own story.

37. This is Jīva Goswāmī's rendering of "Vraja" in GC., *pūrva* 1.15.

38. The killing of Vyomāsura appears in one of the later chapters of the *Bhāgavatam*. Sanātana Goswāmī, however, has rearranged the chronology in such a way that this incident occurs earlier. He has done this with a number of the *Bhāgavatam*'s chapters. He provides evidence to substantiate that the *Bhāgavatam*'s narration is not entirely chronological. Above all, he argues that its narrator, Śukadeva, speaks on the basis of his spiritual ecstasy.

39. The Goswāmīs have demonstrated that although the *Bhāgavatam* describes Kṛṣṇa's birth in Mathurā as the son of Devakī, closer examination of the text reveals that he was born of Yaśodā in Vraja and that the son of Devakī is his expansion. This is confirmed by accounts of Kṛṣṇa's birth in both the *Padma* and *Harivaṁśa Purāṇas*.

40. This happened to Kṛṣṇa's friend Arjuna when Kṛṣṇa demonstrated his Godhood to him in the eleventh chapter of the *Bhagavad-gītā*. Arjuna's love for Kṛṣṇa is of another shade than that of the Vraja gopīs. Even in the face of evidence that Kṛṣṇa is God, the gopīs continue to relate to him as their lover. Such is the power of their love.

41. *muhyanti yat sūrayaḥ* (SB. 1.1.1)

42. Bg. 18.54–55

43. Cc. Antya 16.121–150 paraphrased.

44. This final verse of the chapter is set apart from the others in terms of significance, and thus by its irregular meter as well. It is cited in UN. 14.16 as an example of one of the symptoms of *rūḍha-bhāva*. It is distinguished from the 11th verse of this chapter in that the gopīs are concerned not only with the possibility of Kṛṣṇa's feet incurring pain in the forest, but about the roughness of their breasts when serving as a cushion for his soft soles.

45. Bg. 18.54

46. *Padyāvalī* 14. Trans. by Jan Brzezinski.

47. This is an example of a *daksina-nākiyā*, or right-wing gopī. Their experience of "I am thine" is called *gṛhta-sneha-mayī*. For more details, see UN. 15.93.

48. These are the left-wing gopīs, or *vāmā-nāyikās*, also known as *svādhina-bhartrikā*, or principal *nāyikās*. Their feeling of "He is mine" is known as *madhu-sneha-mayī*. It is further explained in *Ujjvala-nīlamaṇi*.

49. The yogī's trance generally indicates *śānta-rasa*, or neutral love for which the Paramātmā feature of divinity is the object of love (*viṣaya-ālambana-vibhāva*). *Śānta-rasa*, however, is incompatible with conjugal love, or *mādhurya-rasa*. Thus the comparison in this verse must be rendered as above to avoid *rasābhāsa*, incompatibility between *rasas*.

50. The gopīs mentioned here are identified by Sanātana Goswāmī in his *Vaiṣṇava Toṣanī* commentary.

51. *sa vai naiva reme tasmād ekakī na ramāte,* "He does not make love by himself, for one alone has no delight." (Bṛ. U. 1.4.3)

52. (SB. 10.87.23) Also see *Bṛhad-vāmana Purāṇa* and *Sṛṣṭi-khaṇḍa* of *Padma Purāṇa.*

53. *kāmāditaratra tatra cāyatanādibhyaḥ,* "In both the material and spiritual worlds, it is the *parā-śakti* of the Absolute that provides objects of desire for him. This is so because she is all-pervading. She is also the giver of liberation." (Vs. 3.3.40) If the *parā-śakti* was not inherent in the Lord, she could not give liberation. This *śakti* provides objects for the enjoyment of the Absolute by transforming herself. The word *kāmād* indicates that this *śakti* facilitates the erotic sentiment of the Absolute first and foremost and only secondarily facilitates all other sentiments, which are thus subordinate to the erotic.

54. Here the *Bhāgavatam* glorifies *bhāvollasa-rati*, the love of Rādhā's *mañjarī* servant-friends for Rādhā and Kṛṣṇa. This is the vision of Jāhnavā devī, as related in the sixth chapter of *Muralī-vilāsa.* The fact that Rādhā was silent and it was the *mañjarīs* who offered their upper garments for Kṛṣṇa to sit upon is brought out in Jīva Goswāmī's *Gopāla Campū, pūrva campū* 25.12. He directly mentions Rādhā's silence and indirectly mentions the *mañjarīs*, referring to them as "junior girls."

55. Bg. 4.11

56. *yadā paśyaḥ paśyate rukma-varṇaṁ*
kartāram īśaṁ puruṣaṁ brahma-yonim

"One who sees that golden-colored Personality of Godhead, the Supreme Lord, the supreme actor, who is the source of the Supreme Brahman, is liberated." (M.U. 3.1.3.)

ya eva bhagavān kṛṣṇo/ rādhikā-prāṇa-vallabhaḥ/
sṛṣṭy ādau sa jagan-nātho/ gaura āsīn maheśvari//

"The Supreme Person, Śrī Kṛṣṇa himself, who is the life of Śrīmatī Rādhārāṇī and is the Lord of the universe of creation, maintenance, and annihilation, appears as Gaura, O Maheśvarī." *Ananta-saṁhitā*.

57. *Prema-sampuṭikā*. Trans. by Jan Brzezinski.

58. Conjugal love is subdivided into the three categories of *samañjasa, sadharaṇi,* and *samarthā*. Examples of these are the queens of Dvārakā, Kubjā of Mathurā, and the gopīs of Vraja, respectively.

59. In SB. 10.69.2 another example of Kṛṣṇa's capacity to expand himself is cited. This was witnessed by Nārada in Dvārakā. Kṛṣṇa's expansions during the *rāsa* dance are a similar example of this extraordinary capability. Had Kṛṣṇa's ability to expand himself been simply equal to that of yogīs like Nārada, Nārada would not have been astonished.

60. According to *Saṅgītā-sāra*, there are 16,000 principal *rāgas,* all of which were originally manifested during the *rāsa-līlā*.

61. *kathā gānaṁ nāṭyaṁ gamanam,* "The talking of Vraja is song, the walking dance." (Bs. 5. 56)

62. *na vāg gacchati no manaḥ,* "Speech does not go, nor the mind [to Brahman]." (K. U. 1.3)

63. This is an example of boldness in love (*prāgalbhya*).

64. *ānanda-cinmaya-rasa-pratibhāvitābhiḥ* (Bs. 5.37)

65. Bg. 8.17 describes this night to be the duration of one thousand millennium cycles (4,320,000,000 years).

66. Ṛ.V. 10.85.40

CHAPTER THREE

1. The four types of God realization are (1) to live with God (*sālokya*), (2) to acquire opulence like that of God (*sārṣṭi*), (3) to become a personal attendant of God (*sāmīpya*), and (4) to acquire a form like that of God (*sārūpya*). (SB. 3.29.13)

2. Cc. Madhya 25.271

3. This prediction is found in *Caitanya-Bhāgavata,* one of

the authoritative hagiographies on Śrī Caitanya. It states that Śrī Caitanya's name will be sung in every town and village.

4. Swāmī B. R. Śrīdhara Mahārāja, *Śrīmad Bhagavad-gītā: The Hidden Treasure of the Sweet Absolute* (North Yorkshire, UK: The August Assembly, 1988).

5. The general translation reads the opposite, "To favor them I dispel their darkness." Swāmī B. R. Śrīdhara Mahārāja, following Viśvanātha Cakravartī's commentary, however, writes that it may be rendered as above.

6. SB. 10.47.61

7. This explanation of *alaṅkāra* and *dhvani* and how they appear in this verse is from Swāmī B. R. Śrīdhara Mahārāja's *Gītā* commentary.

8. SB. 10.29.12

9. SB. 10.29.15

10. SB. 10.33.39

11. Vs. 1.1.3

12. Cc. Madhya 22.107

13. *viśrambhena guroḥ sevā* (Brs. 1.2.74)

14. *hare kṛṣṇa hare kṛṣṇa, kṛṣṇa kṛṣṇa hare hare, hare rāma hare rāma, rāma rāma hare hare*

15. Ks. U. 1–2

16. Raghunātha dāsa Goswāmī, *Abhīṣta-sūcana*. Trans. by Jan Brzezinski.

17. *vidyā-vadhū jīvanam* (*Śikṣāṣṭakam* 1)

18. See Brs. 1.1.11. At the outset of his treatise, Rūpa Goswāmī has stated that his book is about *uttama-bhakti*. By this he is referring to the path of passionate love. In this verse, the word *ānukūlyena* (favorable) ultimately indicates the service of Rādhā. *Anu* means "to follow," and *kula* means "bound up." One should follow Kṛṣṇa (*ānukūlyena kṛṣṇānuśīlanam*), who is bound up by Rādhā's love.

19. Brs. 1.2.296

20. Bhs. 312

21. *Vaidhi-bhakti* is concerned primarily with *śānta-rasa* and *dāsya-rasa*, with one of Kṛṣṇa's incarnations as the object of love, or with Kṛṣṇa as he appears outside of Vraja, such as in Dvārakā. In the latter instance, all varieties of *bhakti-rasa* are manifest in *aiśvarya-bhāva* (majesty) and the sense of Kṛṣṇa's ultimacy is prominent.

22. SB. 1.2.9

23. SB. 1.2.8

24. Cc. Antya 3.191–193

25. Dhruva Mahārāja (SB. 10.29.10), as per Viśvanātha Cakravartī Ṭhākura's commentary.

26. *ubhaya-vidhaṁ bādarāyaṇaḥ*, "Bādarāyaṇa holds that the liberated are of two types [those with bodies and those without]. (Vs. 4.4.12) Also, *aśva iva romāṇi vidhūya pāpam dhūtvā śarīram akṛtam kṛtātmā brahma-lokam abhisambhavāmi iti*, "Just as a horse shakes off the dust from his body, in the same way I will become free from my karma and attain the spiritual world in a spiritual body (*śarīram akṛtam*). (Ch. U.)

27. SB. 1.6.27–28.

28. The spiritual/emotional body suitable for participation in the *rāsa-līlā* is described in the *Padma Purāṇa* as well as in the *Sanat Kumāra-saṁhitā*.

29. Here I am referring to the reforms of Bhaktisiddhānta Saraswatī Ṭhākura in particular.

30. This is called *bhāvollāsa-rati*, or *rādhā-snehādika*, in which Rādhā along with Kṛṣṇa becomes the object of love and Rūpa Mañjarī the shelter of that love. Following Śrī Rūpa's service in the service of Rādhā-Kṛṣṇa is what the practitioner aspires to. In this expression of *bhakti*, the devotee's love for Rādhā excels his love for Kṛṣṇa. In the *rāsa-pañcādhyaya*, *bhāvollāsa-rati* was highlighted in Kṛṣṇa's confession and submission to the gopīs' love.

31. *śyāmāc chavalaṁ prapadye*
śavalāc chyāmaṁ prapadye

"By surrendering unto black [Kṛṣṇa], one gets white [Rādhā]. By surrendering unto white [Rādhā], one gets black [Kṛṣṇa]. (Ch. U. 8.13.1) *White* also refers to the guru who represents the love of Rādhā. "For receiving the mercy of Kṛṣṇa, I surrender unto his surrender unto Kṛṣṇa."

32. Trans. by Jan Brzezinski.

33. There are three basic divisions of *tad-bhāvecchātmika*: feelings of greater affection for Kṛṣṇa (*kṛṣṇa-snehādika*), equal affection for both Rādhā and Kṛṣṇa (*sama-snehādika*), and greater affection for Rādhā (*rādhā-snehādika*, or *bhāvollāsa*). *Rādhā-snehādika* gopīs are followers of Lalitā Sakhī and Rūpa Mañjarī.

34. Brs. 2.5.101

35. Rādhā-Kṛṣṇa Dāsa Goswāmī, *Daśa-śloki-bhāṣya* (Vṛndāvana, India: Gadādhara-Gaurahari Press, 1982). Trans. by Jan Brzezinski.

36. Brs. 1.2.295

37. SB. 1.1.3

38. SB. 1.2.6

39. Brs. 1.3.1

40. Cc. Madhya 2.50

41. These intensifications of *prema* are *sneha, praṇaya, māna, rāga, anurāga, bhāva,* and *mahābhāva*. The followers of Śrī Rūpa attain *mahābhāva*.

42. Bg. 8.6

43. (Bs. 5.304) This refers to *svābhīṣṭa-bhāva-maya-sādhana*, the principal practice of *rāgānuga*, consisting of identifying oneself as Rādhā's handmaiden and regularly hearing about the love of Rādhā's friends for one another. I have admittedly used it generously here.

44. Rūpa Goswāmī, *Stavamālā*. Trans. by Jan Brzezinski.

Glossary

Acintya-bhedābheda Philosophy of inconceivable oneness and difference.
Āśraya Vessel of love.
Āśraya-ālambana-vibhāva Vessel of the dominant emotion.
Advaita-vedānta Monistic Vedānta.
Anartha Obstacle to devotion.
Anubhāvas Outward symptoms of the dominant emotion.
Avatāra Descent of divinity.
Bhakti Devotion.
Bhakti-rasa Aesthetic experience arising from devotion to Kṛṣṇa.
Bhāva Spiritual emotion.
Brahman Ultimate reality.
Dāsya Divine Servitude.
Devas Gods.
Dharma Religious duty.
Gauḍīya Refers to Śrī Caitanya, who appeared in Gauḍadeśa, West Bengal.
Gopī Cowherd girl.
Jñāna Knowledge.
Kāma Lust.
Kīrtana Song in praise of God.
Līlā Divine play.
Mādhurya The sweetness of conjugal love.
Mahā-bhāva The most intense stage of love of Kṛṣṇa.
Mañjarīs Associated servant-friends of Rādhā and Kṛṣṇa.
Māyā śakti External energy.

Pārakīyā Paramour love.
Paramātmā Indwelling guide.
Prema The highest spiritual love.
Rāga Attachment.
Rāgānuga-bhakti The path of passionate love.
Rāgātmikas Those in whom *rāga* is inborn.
Rasa Aesthetic rapture.
Rāsa-līlā The circular love dance of Rādhā and Kṛṣṇa.
Rāsa-pañcādhyāya The five chapters of *Bhāgavatam* relating the love dance of Rādhā-Kṛṣṇa and the gopīs.
Rasa-rāja King of aesthetic rapture.
Rasika Connoisseur of aesthetic rapture.
Rati Love.
Sādhaka Practitioner.
Sādhaka-deha External spiritualized body of the practitioner.
Sādhana The path of spiritual practice.
Sādhya The goal of spiritual practice.
Sakhya Fraternal love of God.
Śakti Energy of God.
Samartha-rati Competent love.
Saṁsāra Cycle of birth and death.
Saṁskāras Latent impressions formed in previous lives.
Śānta Passive love of God.
Sāttvika-bhāvas Involuntary ecstasies.
Siddha-deha Perfect spiritual body.
Śruti Upaniṣads.
Sthāyi-bhāva Dominant emotion.
Svarūpa śakti Internal energy of God.

Tatastha śakti Marginal energy of God.
Tulasī Sacred basil tree.
Uddīpana-vibhāvas Excitants that stimulate the dominant emotion.
Vaidhi-bhakti Ritualistic devotion.
Vaiṣṇava Devotee of Viṣṇu.
Vātsalya Parental love of God.
Vedānta Concluding portion of the Vedas.
Vibhāvas Determinants or casual factors in the production of *rasa*.
Viṣaya Object of love.
Viṣaya-ālambana-vibhāva Object to which the dominant emotion is directed.
Vraja Kṛṣṇa's land of love.
Vyabhicāri-bhāvas Fleeting auxiliary emotions.

Bibliography

Brzezenski, Jan. *Gopalā Campu*. Eugene, OR: Clarion Call Publishing, forthcoming.

Dāsa, Kuñjabihārī. *Mañjarī-svarūpa-nirūpaṇa*, trans. Jan Brzezenski, unpublished.

Delmonico, Neal. *A Study of the Religious Aesthetic of Rupa Goswami*. Ann Arbor: UMI, 1996.

Ghoshal, Dr. S. N. *Rasacandrikā and Studies in Divine Aesthetics*. Santiniketan: Satischandra Sen, 1969.

Haberman, David L. *Acting as a Way of Salvation: A Study of Rāgānugā Bhakti Sādhana*. New York: Oxford University Press, 1988.

Hawley, J. S., and D. M. Wulff. *The Divine Consort: Rādhā and the Goddesses of India*. Boston: Beacon Press, 1982.

Ingalls, D. H. H., J. M. Masson, and M. V. Patwardhan. *The Dhvanyāloka of Ānandavardhana*. Cambridge, Massachusetts: Harvard University Press, 1990.

Kapoor, O. B. L. *Religion and Philosophy of Sri Caitanya*. New Delhi: Munshiram Manoharalal Publishers, 1976.

———. *Sri Caitanya and Raganuga Bhakti*. Vrindavan: The Vaishnava Book Trust, 1995.

Kinsley, David R. *The Sword and the Flute: Kālī and Kṛṣṇa, Dark Visions of the Terrible and the Sublime in Hindu Mythology*. Berkeley: University of California, 1975.

Maharaja, Bon. *Bhakti-rasāmṛta-sindhu*. Vrindavan: Institute of Oriental Philosophy, 1965.

Masson, J. L., and M. V. Patwardhan *Aesthetic Rapture: The Rasādhyaya of the Nāṭyśāstra,* Vols. 1 & 2. Poona: Deccan College, 1970.

Radhakrishnan, S. *The Principal Upaniṣads*. New Delhi: Indus, 1994.

Redington James D. S. J. *Vallabhācārya on the Love Games of Kṛṣṇa*. New Delhi: Motilala Banarsidass Publishers, 1983.

Sastri, Haridasa. *Bhakti-sandarbha of Jīva Goswāmī*. Vrindavan: Śrī Gadādhara Gaurahari Press, 1986.

———. *Priti-sandarbha of Jīva Goswāmī*. Vrindavan: Śrī Gadādhara Gaurahari Press, 1986.

———. *Vedānta Darṣanam*. Vrindavan: Śrī Gadādhara Gaurahari Press, 1980.

Sax, William S. *The Gods at Play: Līlā in South Asia*. New York: Oxford University Press, 1995.

Śrīdhara, Bhakti Rakṣaka *Śrīmad Bhagavad Gītā: Hidden Treasure of the Sweet Absolute*. Navadwip Dham: Dayādhara Gauraṅga, 1986.

Srisa Candra Vasu, Rai Bahadur. *The Vedānta Sūtras of Bādarāyaṇa with the Commentary of Baladeva*. New Delhi: Oriental Books Reprint Corporation, 1979.

Swami, A. C. Bhaktivedanta. *Kṛṣṇa: The Supreme Personality of Godhead*. Los Angles: Bhaktivedanta Book Trust, 1970.

———. *Nectar of Devotion*. Los Angeles: Bhaktivedanta Book Trust, 1970.

———. *Śrī Caitanya-caritamṛta*. Los Angeles: Bhakti–vedanta Book Trust, 1975.

———. *Śrīmad-Bhāgavatam*. New South Wales: Bhaktivedanta Book Trust, 1988.

Thakura, Bhaktisiddhanta Saraswati. *Śrī Brahma-saṁhitā*. Los Angeles: Bhaktivedanta Book Trust, 1985.

Thakura, Bhaktivinoda. *Jaiva Dharma*. Madras: Sri Gaudiya Math, 1994.

———. *Shri Chaitanya Siksāmritam*. Madras: Sri Gaudiya Math, 1983.

Tripurāri, Swāmī B. V. *Jīva Goswāmi's Tattva-sandarbha: Sacred India's Philosophy of Ecstasy*. Eugene: Clarion Call Publishing, 1996.

Wulff, Donna M. *Drama as a Mode of Religious Realization: the Vidagdhamādhava of Rūpa Goswāmī*. Chico, CA: Scholars Press, 1984.

Yati, Bhakti Prajnan. *Śrīmad-Bhāgavatam*. Madras: Sri Gaudiya Math, 1966.

———. *Twelve Essential Upanishads*. Madras: Sri Gaudiya Math, 1984.